Home Makeovers That Sell

Home Makeovers That Sell

Quick and Easy Ways to Get the Highest Possible Price

Sid Davis

AMACOM

American Management Association

New York • Atlanta • Brussels • Chicago • Mexico City • San Francisco
Shanghai • Tokyo • Toronto • Washington, D.C.

Special discounts on bulk quantities of AMACOM books are available to corporations, professional associations, and other organizations. For details, contact Special Sales Department, AMACOM, a division of American Management Association, 1601 Broadway, New York, NY 10019.
Tel: 212-903-8316. Fax: 212-903-8083.
E-mail: specialsls@amanet.org
Website: www. amacombooks.org/go/specialsales
To view all AMACOM titles go to: www.amacombooks.org

This publication is designed to provide accurate and authoritative information in regard to the subject matter covered. It is sold with the understanding that the publisher is not engaged in rendering legal, accounting, or other professional service. If legal advice or other expert assistance is required, the services of a competent professional person should be sought.

REALTOR® is a registered collective membership mark that identifies a real estate professional who is a member of the National Association of REALTORS® and subscribes to its strict Code of Ethics. AMACOM uses this term throughout this book in initial capital letters or ALL CAPITAL letters for editorial purposes only, with no intention of trademark violation.

Library of Congress Cataloging-in-Publication Data

Davis, Sid.
    Home makeovers that sell : quick and easy ways to get the highest possible price / Sid Davis.
        p. cm.
    Includes bibliographical references and index.
    ISBN-10: 0-8144-7373-3
    ISBN-13: 978-0-8144-7373-3
    1. House selling—United States. 2. Dwellings—Maintenance and repair.
I. Title.

HD259.D367 2007
643'.120973—dc22   2006016396

Printing Number

10 9 8 7 6 5 4 3 2 1

Contents

PREFACE   vii

CHAPTER 1. Finding Your Home's Highest Sales Price   1

CHAPTER 2. Take Control: Decluttering 101   23

CHAPTER 3. Cleaning for Dollars   42

CHAPTER 4. Repairs/Upgrades That Make or Cost You
            Money   56

CHAPTER 5. Upgrading Your Home's Exterior   75

CHAPTER 6. Putting Your Landscaping in Selling Condition   91

CHAPTER 7. Showtime: Pulling It All Together   104

CHAPTER 8. Marketing Your Home for a Quick Offer   120

CHAPTER 9. Working with Offers and Counteroffers   142

CHAPTER 10. Solving Difficult Selling Problems   158

CHAPTER 11. Showcasing: How the Pros Do It 174

APPENDIX 1. Tax Aspects of Making Over Your Home and
Selling It 187

APPENDIX 2. The Seven Dumbest Mistakes Sellers Make 197

INDEX 209

Preface

Most people would be really upset if their retirement account suddenly dropped ten, twenty, thirty thousand dollars, or more. Yet many homeowners willingly suffer these kinds of losses without a whimper when they sell their home. And too often, that's because they fail to perceive their homes as an important investment as well as shelter for themselves, their dog and goldfish.

For the vast homeowning majority, building home equity is a critical component of retirement planning and building net worth. So, it only makes sense to get the most money possible when you sell. Those extra thousands of dollars can give you a bigger down payment on your next home, capital for a business venture, or money to fund some other investment.

The first (and most critical) step in selling your home for top dollar is to develop a simple plan of action and give yourself enough time to implement it. In other words, don't do as so many home sellers do when they decide to sell: plant a "For Sale" sign in the turf and wait for a buyer to come with an open checkbook.

True, this can work in a hot market—and possibly you'll sell your home fast this way. But chances are you'll leave a lot of money on the table and give the buyer something to brag about at the office.

Fortunately, there's a different approach that will net you thousands of dollars more than your uninformed neighbor. It's not difficult or expensive, it just requires paying attention to detail and implementing the plan of action this book lays out for you.

The first chapter covers how to determine the highest asking price for your home—and no, that's not like solving a two-page-long math problem. It just takes some easy, commonsense homework. Once you've settled on a price, the next five chapters cover in detail how to present your home. Also included are tips and warnings that help you anticipate and avoid costly problems that trip up unwary home sellers. In addition, you will find especially valuable insider tips and techniques, which most real estate agents don't even know, that will help supersize your closing check.

It's often said that it's the packaging that sells the product and Chapter 7 ties the previous chapters together. It shows you how to showcase your home so you get full-price offers; you may even have to mediate a bidding war among several buyers.

Chapter 8 shows you how to work with multiple offers, low offers, concessions, and when and how to counter an offer—or when to simply say, "No!" This chapter also covers repair addendums and other sticky eleventh-hour problems that can jeopardize the sale when you're most vulnerable.

Finally, Chapter 9 is a problem-solving chapter. It covers how to solve many common and sticky problems that take the fun out of real estate, such as taxes, divorce, bankruptcy, short sales, and payments in arrears. The appendices also address these types of problems. And there's even a roundup appendix that spotlights the seven biggest mistakes sellers make when selling their home. It's like a handy checklist you'll want to refer to as you progress through the selling process.

But in the end, the goal of the book is to make sure you walk out of closing with a check that hasn't suffered the fate of a new cotton T-shirt run through the hot water cycle.

CHAPTER 1

Finding Your Home's Highest Sales Price

Few homeowners sell their homes for the most money possible. They end up giving thousands of dollars to the buyers as equity gifts.

Why do so many sellers end up with less money than they should have? It's usually because they don't do a little commonsense prep work. They don't do what many car owners do when it's time to sell: clean the car inside and out so it's attractive, showcase it so it looks its best, and promote it by making available its repair and oil change records. The owner may even copy the page in a used car value guide that documents for a buyer what the car is worth. Nothing is left to chance; no stone is left unturned in the quest for the best price possible.

But interestingly, few homeowners are willing to do what it takes when their home is involved and thousands of dollars are on the line, not a few hundred.

To put it bluntly, if homeowners followed the same route selling their home as a savvy car owner would selling a 1999 Honda Accord, they would end up depositing thousands of dollars more a lot faster.

With that said, the rest of this chapter focuses on giving you the tools to price your home at the top of the market. If you work with an agent, you'll know how the pricing game is played and can make sure you get the best price.

Don't Jump into the Game Before You've Done Some Homework

Both Maria and Don were thrilled when he got a job offer on the West Coast. His company had downsized and similar jobs were hard to find locally. Plus, it meant a big salary increase. It also meant selling their home as soon as possible.

Maria had a close friend, Andrea, who had just gotten her real estate license. Maria called her and asked if she could come by and list the house.

Andrea came that evening and told Maria and Don that they should get top price because the home was decorated so nicely. They had upgraded the two bathrooms and replaced the carpets and kitchen counters.

When they asked Andrea what price they should go with, she wasn't entirely comfortable recommending one. Don recalled that a home up the street sold about two months ago for $290,000, but it wasn't decorated nearly as nicely as theirs. Marie then suggested that it would be nice to recoup the $15,000 they spent on upgrades. They would also need about $100,000 for the down payment and closing costs to get into another home in a much more expensive area. After kicking it around for a while, they agreed to try $360,000. Andrea assured them it would sell quickly because it was such a cute house.

Don took the job offer and he and Maria planned an extended weekend trip to scout out their new city and find a home since they only had about thirty days.

The first week was hectic. Andrea put the home on the local multiple listing service (MLS), printed some flyers for a brochure box attached to the "For Sale" sign, and scheduled open houses for the weekend. Everyone felt sure the home would sell the first week or two.

Buyers are more savvy than ever about home values. Many access websites like *Realtor.com, forsalebyowner.com* and pour over MLS printouts before they start to look at neighborhoods and homes for sale. As a result, if you're overpriced, they know it and you end up helping the competition sell their homes.

Four weeks went by and nothing much happened. Although Andrea refilled the brochure box several times, there were few calls from the flyers or other Realtors on the MLS. "Maybe it's just slow getting started," Andrea told Maria, during one of her many phone calls.

By the end of the sixth week, showings from agents picked up, but time was running out and Don had to leave for his new job. It was decided that Maria would have to stay behind until the house sold.

Two months passed and the stress was intense. It was exhausting keeping the home in showing condition, baking cookies to make the home smell good, and wondering why the home wasn't selling. Maria was getting tired of Andrea's excuses: the market was cooling off, interest rates were going up, and so on. It was fast becoming a panic situation.

One afternoon, when an agent brought some buyers to see the home, Maria was running a little late leaving. As she walked to the garage, she overheard the agent telling his clients that the home was clearly overpriced and that he had a similar home for sale two streets over for $40,000 less. The agent also told the buyers he was only showing them the home so they could see what a good deal the others on the list were.

Maria was shocked. Then reality slowly dawned. Agents were using her home to sell other homes. All those showings . . . Anger replaced shock as Maria called the real estate office number on the lawn sign. She tried to remain civil to the receptionist, but when the broker picked up the call, she lost it.

Luckily, the broker was a professional and listened until Maria ran out of steam and calmed down. By that time, she had Maria's file in front of her and explained that she was not personally familiar with the hundreds of listings the company had. But she promised to look into it and get back to her before the end of the day.

After calling Andrea into her office, the broker realized that her agent had not done a comparative market analysis (CMA) and this was her first listing. In fact, Andrea was clueless about how to work up an accurate CMA.

Normally, the broker would have assigned a seasoned agent to help out a green agent on their first listing, but somehow that had fallen through the cracks.

Early the next day, Maria's listing was assigned to Brad, one of the companies top agents, to salvage the situation and see what could be done to sell the house. The first thing Brad did was pull up all the similar homes that had sold in the area the past sixty days as well as all homes that were now on the market—in other words, the competition.

It became apparent immediately that the home was overpriced by $40,000 to $45,000 and the yard needed some landscaping work to bring up the curb appeal.

Don and Maria hired a landscaper to improve the yard and reduced the price $47,000 to stimulate a fast sale. As a result, the home sold in about two weeks.

What Should You Do?

1. Do some pricing homework on your own first, even if you plan on going with an agent. It's important to have an accurate idea of what your home is worth. This entails looking at similar homes on the market in the area, stopping by open houses, checking out county recorder's records of recent sales, or having a real estate agent print out sold comparables from the MLS. A later section tells you how to do this.

2. Pick your agent carefully, you have hundreds of thousands of dollars at stake. Would you let your novice cousin manage your 401(k) or investment portfolio? Probably not! So talk to two or three agents and go with the one who has the best track record in your area.

3. Find out what the average days on market (DOM) is for your area and home style. If it is thirty days or less, you're in a hot market and can plan on a fast sale. But if it is running sixty days plus, make

your plans accordingly and don't paint yourself into a corner with unrealistic expectations.

4. Don't put your home on the market before you've put it in top selling condition. Follow the action plans in this book so you'll get top dollar faster. If your home languishes on the market more than a few weeks, you'll attract bargain hunters who never pay full price for anything.

5. Insist that your agent call the buyer's agents who are showing the home to get their client's feedback. If you don't get an offer from them, you want to know why.

> Cut to the chase and eliminate hype when you interview agents to list your home. Ask them for MLS printouts of their last ten sold listings. Note the days on market (DOM), list price, and sales price. A top agent will be happy to give you this data.

What Determines a Home's Value?

When it comes down to the nitty-gritty, your home is worth what someone is willing to pay for it. In a super hot market with several buyers bidding against each other, the value can escalate in minutes to thousands of dollars over the starting price. In fact, buyers in some markets know they have to start thousands of dollars over asking price just to play in the game. Buying a home can get ugly as more buyers chase fewer properties in a market that seems to increasingly defy gravity.

In a normal market where the numbers of buyers and sellers are more balanced and homes aren't selling before the seller finishes pounding a sign in the turf, the usual valuation rules apply. The five most important are:

1. Location is the most important component of a home's value. The better the location, the quicker a home sells and for a higher price. In many areas smaller, older homes sell for unusually high prices because buyers can tear them down and build much larger homes.

Location is the engine the drives these "tear-downs" and seller windfalls.

2. The condition of a home, of course, is important. The more a home tugs at the buyer's emotional strings, the more money a seller walks away with. Conversely, a home that isn't cared for will attract bargain hunters and sell for a big discount.

3. How hot the local market is has a big effect on the selling game. If there are more buyers than sellers, prices go up; the greater the imbalance, the faster homes appreciate. It's also a double-edged sword. If you turn around and buy another home in the same market, you'll also end up paying more and that tends to swallow your big gain. On the other hand, if you were to move from Boston to Ottumwa, Iowa you would be able to upgrade your housing lifestyle considerably. It's probably accurate to say that owning a home in the right place at the right time can add a big windfall to your net worth.

4. Competition comes in many forms and can change quickly. For instance, a new subdivision next to you may siphon off buyers; a large, congestion-causing box store or highway re-route close to your neighborhood may lower home values. Also, there may be more homes for sale than buyers in your area at the time you want to sell. And there are interest rates and other economic factors outside of your control always lurking in the background that will affect your market.

5. Of course, price is a big part of selling a home and you have to stay within your neighborhood value range. But sometimes the gap between the lowest-priced home and the highest-priced home in an area can be as wide as the Grand Canyon, and that spells opportunity. It means you have more leeway to create emotional appeal and get top dollar for your home than if all the homes were roughly the same size and age.

Unfortunately, if a home isn't selling, too many agents take the lazy route and tell the owner their price is too high when a few improvements could make a big difference. This leads to a downward price spiral until eventually the home sells and the homeowners lose several thousand dollars they didn't have to. Incidentally, this is the situation this book strives to prevent in the coming chapters.

All of these home-selling economic components, and many sub-components, are in constant play. When you put your home on the market, it's like shooting at a moving target; conditions are constantly changing. Can you price it a little high or will that slow down the sale? Will replacing the carpet help sell it or will it be wasted equity? The next sections show how different approaches are typically used to establish a sales price.

How Appraisers Value Your Home

Establishing a sales price is far from an exact science, and that's probably due to the many emotional factors in play. A good example of this is when several buyers try to outbid each other over a home in a desirable area or one that has a lot of emotional appeal. What is the home's real value? Many would say it's the highest bid. In reality, a home is worth what someone is willing to pay for it, subject to the bank's approval if a mortgage is involved. And it's at this point that professional appraisers and Fannie Mae come on stage to run the show.

Fannie Mae is the overwhelming heavyweight on the house-buying playground. It's a big public corporation that buys mortgages from most of the banks who make the home loans. Chances are it'll be their software that crunches the numbers and data on your mortgage application and tells the lender how much you can afford and what your interest rate will be.

Since Fannie Mae has the gold, it's not surprising that they also set the rules and guidelines for the bank's appraisers and require their forms be used in submitting an appraisal. You would think that this

If an appraisal comes in lower than your sales price, you or your agent can contest the appraisal by finding comparable homes that have sold in the last ninety days. You'll need to take care that your comparables fit within the appraisal guidelines outlined below.

would all bring consistency and accuracy to the process. Unfortunately, this is not always so. Being the imperfect world it is, there is a dark side to the appraisal process. Paydays for appraisers come from mortgage lenders. No loan, no payday. The temptation is high to make the lenders, real estate agents, buyers, and sellers happy so they keep you in the loop for future jobs.

As a result of all this, a significant number of loans have been granted based on inflated appraisals. Of course, the foreclosure rate on these loans is much higher and that costs the rest of us in higher fees and private mortgage insurance (PMI) premiums.

On the positive side, the vast majority of appraisers are professionals who want to do the most accurate job they can. For the most part, their appraisals are fair and reflect the current market values. However, it's important to realize that appraisers are humans, they all have different tastes, different ways of looking at the same data, and different levels of experience. And some have a greater range in their numbers than others.

Because of this, you need to do a little homework and look at similar homes that have sold so you have a ballpark feeling for what your home is worth. This entails about the same amount of time you would spend researching a price if you were selling a 1999 Honda.

In one home sale, for example, the appraisal came back right on the sales price. However, a few days later the buyer ran into trouble and fell short of the $4,500 needed for the down payment and closing costs. Rather than let the deal fall through, the buyer's agent contacted the listing agent, told him the problem, and asked if they could do an addendum adding $4,500 to the sale price. The sellers would then cover that amount as a sales concession.

However, before the sellers agreed, their agent contacted the appraiser and asked him if he could increase the appraisal by the amount of the concession. He agreed and the deal closed.

Does this mean the home was underpriced? Not necessarily. The selling process had gone back and forth with offers and counters over several days. If the sellers had priced the home $4,500 higher, the buyers wouldn't even have considered the home.

But once they started working out the deal, the buyer's thinking changed to, what do we need to do to make this work?

Does it mean the appraiser came in low? Again, not necessarily. When the request came in for an increase, the appraiser looked at the data and the market. He felt the market was going up so it wouldn't be a problem to increase the price so the deal could close.

Would another appraiser have gone along with this request? Some would, others wouldn't. Remember, appraisers are human and they all form judgments based on likes, dislikes, experience, and training.

The lesson to be gleaned from all this is that the sales and appraisal process is elastic. It's like a rubber band; you don't know how far it will stretch until you try it. The key is to go into the deal using the best data available and keep your thinking flexible.

It helps to know what guidelines the appraisers use when you're out there looking for comparables. Since Fannie Mae is the elephant in the room, it's best to use their appraisal guidelines. Six of the most important ones are:

1. The comparable homes should be within one mile of your home.
2. The sold date should not be more than six months.
3. The square footage above grade should be within 200 square feet of your home.
4. The comparables should range in age plus or minus five years of your home's age.
5. The style should be the same as your home. For example, Cape Cod compared with Cape Cod, trilevel compared with trilevel, and so on.
6. The comparable sold properties should be from the same or a close competing neighborhood.

If you have a unique home and can't find comparables or there haven't been enough recent sales in your area, you may want to spend

If you're having trouble finding comparables on your own, don't try to wing it. Spend a few hundred dollars to hire a professional appraiser. They have the skills and tools to come up an accurate sales price.

$350 to $400 and hire a professional appraiser. Make sure the appraiser is licensed in your state and is on the list of most mortgage lenders in your area. When you sell your home, the buyer's lender can use the appraisal for their loan, and you should get credit on the closing statement for the appraisal cost.

Figure 1 shows the comparison section of a residential appraisal. Notice that the first two columns are labeled *item* and *subject*, listing all of the amenities of the subject home. The other three columns, labeled *comparables 1*, *2*, and *3* compares three properties amenity by

Figure 1. Uniform Residential Appraisal Report.

Valuation Section — **UNIFORM RESIDENTIAL APPRAISAL REPORT** — **File No. 05-463**

COST APPROACH

ESTIMATED SITE VALUE	= $	90,000
ESTIMATED REPRODUCTION COST-NEW-OF IMPROVEMENTS:		
Dwelling 1,163 Sq. Ft. @$ 125.00	= $	145,375
400 Sq. Ft. @$ 20.00	= $	8,000
Appl, Porch, Deck, Upgrades	= $	20,000
Garage/Carport Sq. Ft. @$ 20.00	= $	
Total Estimated Cost New	= $	173,375
Less Depreciation: Physical 43,375; Functional; External	= $	43,375
Depreciated Value of Improvements	= $	130,000
"As-Is"Value of Site Improvements	= $	10,000
INDICATED VALUE BY COST APPROACH	= $	230,000

Comment on Cost Approach (such as, source of cost estimate, site value, square foot calculation and for HUD, VA and FmHA, the estimated remaining economic life of the property): **Site value is based on review of recent land sale and site-to-value ratios—high but typical for the neighborhood. Cost approach data was taken from Marshall & Swift Cost Handbook & modified to the local market using cost & location modifiers. Local contractors were also consulted when available. Physical depreciation is based on the age/life method.**

SALES COMPARISON ANALYSIS

ITEM	SUBJECT	COMPARABLE NO. 1		COMPARABLE NO. 2		COMPARABLE NO. 3	
Address	187 N. Salt Lake City	681 E. Salt Lake City		335 N. Salt Lake City		583 E. Salt Lake City	
Proximity to Subject		0.11 miles		0.33 miles		0.28 miles	
Sales Price	$ 230,000		$ 239,000		$ 227,500		$ 226,500
Price/Gross Living Area	$ 197.75	$ 197.20		$ 251.66		$ 173.21	
Data and/or Verification Source	Inspection	MLS CLOSED SALE #530357		MLS CLOSED SALE #541071		MLS CLOSED SALE #535823	
VALUE ADJUSTMENTS	DESCRIPTION	DESCRIPTION	+/(−)$ Adjust.	DESCRIPTION	+/(−)$ Adjust.	DESCRIPTION	+/(−)$ Adjust.
Sales or Financing Concessions		CONV Pts Paid	−5,000	CONV Pts Paid	−500	CONV None Reported	
Date of Sale/Time		9-7-05		10-6-05		9-15-05	
Location	Good	Good		Good		Good	
Leasehold/Fee Simple	Fee Simple	Fee Simple		Fee Simple		Fee Simple	
Site	.09 ac	.09 ac		.07 ac		.09 ac	
View	Average	Average		Average		Average	
Design and Appeal	Rambler/Avg	Rambler/Avg		Rambler/Avg		Rambler/Avg	
Quality of Construction	BV/Avg	BV/AVE		BV/Avg		Stc/Avg	
Age	115 yrs	105 yrs		97 yrs		101 yrs	
Condition	Good/Remodel	Good/Remodel		Good/Remodel		Good/Remodel	
Above Grade Room Count (Total / Bdrms / Baths)	5 / 2 / 1	5 / 3 / 1		4 / 2 / 1		5 / 2 / 1	
Gross Living Area	1,163 Sq. Ft.	1,210 Sq. Ft.	−1,100	904 Sq. Ft.	+5,200	1,310 Sq. Ft.	−2,900
Basement & Finished Rooms Below Grade	400 s.f. Unfin	350 s.f. Unfin	0	145 s.f. Unfin	+300	None Unfin	+500
Functional Utility	Average	Average		Average		Average	
Heating/Cooling	FWA/Central	FWA/W AC	+1,500	FRW/Central		FWA/W-Evap	+1,500
Energy Efficient Items	Average	Average		Average		Average	
Garage/Carport	none	None		1-Garage	−2,500	None	
Porch, Patio, Deck, Fireplace, etc.	Porch, Deck 1-WYS	Porch 1-Fireplace	+1,000	Porch, Patio 1-Fireplace		Porch, Patio 1-Fireplace	
Fence, Pool, etc.	Avg Landscape	Avg Landscape		Avg Landscape		Avg Landscape	
	Kitchen Appl	Kitchen Appl		Kitchen Appl		Kitchen Appl	
Net Adj. (total)		☐ + ☒ −	$ 3,600	☒ + ☐ −	$ 2,500	☐ + ☒ −	$ 900
Adjusted Sales Price of Comparable		Net 1.5 % Gross 3.5 %	$ 236,300	Net 1.1 % Gross 3.7 %	$ 230,000	Net 0.4 % Gross 2.2 %	$ 226,000

Comments on Sales Comparison (including the subject property's compatibility to the neighborhood, etc.): **All 3 sales are similar in location and utility. Adjustments were made to reflect differences in financing concessions, size, car storage, A/C, patios/decks. The sales used were the most recent, closest in location, and best available. They support and bracket the final estimate of value.**

amenity. Where the match isn't exact, plus or minus dollar adjustments are made.

In this case, the home's $230,000 sales price is closely bracketed by the comparables the appraiser found on the local multiple listing service and the appraisal came in right on.

Unfortunately, it's not always this easy. Sometimes other homes in the neighborhood are not similar enough to be good comparables. In this case, the appraiser may have to go with replacement or reproduction cost, less depreciation. If you've got the smallest home in the area, you'll benefit by the area's higher average value. It costs a lot more to replace your home in a good neighborhood than it does in a not-so-good location. This is why Realtors say location is the most important consideration when buying a home. Or in other words, your neighbors' homes influence what your home is worth and what it'll sell for.

How Realtors Value Your Home

Experienced agents typically value a home by putting together a comparative market analysis (CMA). They use not only data from the same sold properties an appraiser would use, but go a little further and use competitive properties in the area and those that are under contract but haven't closed yet. Sometimes agents will include homes that didn't sell and their listings have expired—something that doesn't happen too often in a hot market, but can be important data in a slower market.

Because CMAs can be more proactive than an appraisal, they look at what's currently for sale and what has recently sold but not yet closed. With this data, a good agent can anticipate where the market is going and price a home at the top to get the most money possible.

Appraisals, on the other hand tend to be reactive. The appraiser ends up trying to justify the price a buyer has agreed to pay for a home by using past sales and/or replacement costs. In a hot market, this can put the data behind the curve.

The bottom line to this argument is that an experienced agent familiar with a neighborhood can usually price a home to get the maximum price possible by anticipating the market. Plus, the time it takes for a home to sell and close can mean several thousand dollars more to the home seller in a market that's going up like there's no gravity.

There's a caveat in the above paragraph that kicks us back to the beginning of the chapter: To get an accurate pricing for your home, you need to go with an experienced agent who has a track record in your area. Otherwise, their CMA won't be worth a cold cheeseburger.

So how do you pick a good agent? Here are some tips that'll help narrow it down:

HOW TO PICK A GOOD AGENT

WHAT TO LOOK FOR	TIPS
Experience	Since the agent is going to handle your biggest investment, you want to choose him with the same care you would take in choosing a financial planner, or for some of us, a veterinarian. Listing with an inexperienced relative or friend can cost you money and create hard feelings.
Track Record	Ask the agent for a printout of her last ten to twelve sales in your area. Note the days on market and list price to sales price. The local superstar may not be your best bet if she is too busy to work with you. A consistent agent with two or three sales a month in your area can be a good choice.
Area Experience	This is important because neighborhoods are different and values can change just by crossing the street. You want one experienced in your area.
Easy to Work With	This is important. If an agent never returns your phone calls, it can get frustrating fast. Ask for two or three past clients you can call for references.
Designations	Lots of initials on the agent's card such CRS (Certified Residential Specialist) and other professional attainments are good, but are not a guarantee he is the best choice, though they are a good place to start.
Referred to You	If someone has used this agent and liked her, it's a plus. Still, look at the total picture before committing.

How You Can Determine What Your Home Is Worth

As previously stressed, before you talk to agents about listing your home or getting an appraisal, it's important to get a good idea of what your home is worth on your own. Several ways you can do this are:

- In some counties you can look up homes that have sold recently and the sales price is disclosed. Other states, namely, Idaho, Indiana, Iowa, Kansas, Missouri, New Mexico, Texas, Utah, and Wyoming are nondisclosure states. Sales prices are not disclosed when data is recorded. Try going to www.co.(your county).(your state).us/recorder. Counties will sometimes charge to use their site, while others are free. You can also call your county recorder or pay them a visit.

- Find your title policy from when you bought your home, call the title company that issued it and ask for customer service. Since you're selling and will need to buy title insurance soon, your previous insurer should do handsprings to keep you happy.

- If you bought your home through an agent, ask him or her to print out a list of recent sales in your area. In return, you'll put that agent on your short list when you get ready to interview.

- Visit open houses that are similar to yours and located in your area.

- Call on "For Sale" signs in your neighborhood and keep track of how fast they sell. Don't be bashful about calling the owner who has sold but not closed. Tell him you're thinking of selling and ask him what his sold for. Most sellers are glad to help a fellow homeowner.

- If your home is unique or there haven't been any sales the past several months, you may want to spend $300 to $400 for a professional appraisal. In a hot market, it's a good idea to price the home a few thousand dollars over the appraisal to "lead the target." You'll know you priced your home too high if you get three or four qualified buyers through and they don't come back for a second look or make offers.

It's important to note that the agent you used to buy your home is not necessarily your best choice for selling it. If you find in your interviews that another agent is more familiar with your area and has a better track record of homes which have sold, he or she is probably the agent you'll want to go with.

Tips for Checking Out the Competition

The form in Figure 2 will give you a good feel for what your home is worth. To use the worksheet, fill in the columns with three sold properties and three competing properties that are similar to yours. Be as objective as possible and add or subtract dollars for each amenity that differs from your home.

Figure 2. Comparison Worksheet.

	Your Home	Sold #1	Sold #2	Sold #3	For Sale #1	For Sale #2	For Sale #3
Address							
Price							
Neighborhood							
Home Style							
Square Footage							
Exterior							
Roof Condition							
Gutters							
Drainage							
Kitchen							
Upgrades							
Baths							
Family Room							
Fireplaces							
Laundry							
Driveway							
Landscaping							
Curb Appeal							
Schools							
± Compared to Your Home							
Estimated Value of Your Home							

For example, if most of the similar homes on the market in your area have updated their kitchen appliances, countertops, and cabinets and you haven't, then you'll need to make a minus entry in your home's column. If the average cost is $15,000 for a kitchen upgrade, you may have to price your home less to compensate, but not necessarily the full amount. For example:

TYPICAL COSTS FOR KITCHEN UPGRADES

ITEM	ESTIMATED COST
Vinyl, wood, or tile floors	$1,500 to $4,500
Laminate, tile, or granite countertops	$2,000 to $6,500
Cabinets—refinish replace hardware	$200 to $500
Cabinets—new doors and hardware	$750 to $1,500
Cabinets—replace	$2,500 to $12,000
Upgrade appliances: range, dishwasher, refrigerator	$2,200 to $2,800
Sink and faucet	$150 to $700
Lighting fixtures	$90 to $300

In *Remodeling* magazine's 2005 "cost versus value" annual report, they say the average cost a homeowner will recover from an upgraded kitchen is 98.5 percent. However, this figure can vary even from neighborhood to neighborhood. Homes in some hot areas typically recover as much as 150 percent of the cost.

The best way to find the value effect of specific upgrades in your area is to look for comparable homes that have sold "as is," and homes that were upgraded, and note the difference in sales price. You can also use this approach to find out how local amenities such as schools, public transportation access, medical care facilities, shopping, and so on affect pricing. While you're at it, check out the days on market (DOM) of homes for sale in your area.

For example, when Alex and JoLynn decided to sell their 2,400-square-foot trilevel, they used a worksheet similar to Figure 2 to get an idea of how to price their home. With the help of the agent who sold them their home five years ago, they got a list of eleven similar homes that recently sold in their area. Two of the homes were on their

Sometimes using comparables isn't enough. In a hot market, you have to factor in the number of homes for sale and the monthly appreciation rate. That can up your price many thousands of dollars.

street and they had been in them before they sold. Both had comparable upgraded kitchens and floor coverings. One sold for $278,300 and the other for $279,750. One of the other homes on the list was two streets over, had not been upgraded, was on the market two weeks longer than the others, and sold for $261,900.

Driving around on a weekend, Alex and JoLynn noticed that two homes in their subdivision had open houses going so they stopped in. The first, priced at $299,500, was beautifully decorated with new carpets and muted green walls accented with white base and crown molding. In addition, the kitchen was upgraded with all new appliances and granite countertops. Obviously, this home was the nicest in the area and priced at the top of the market. However, it had been on the market for nearly two weeks with no offers.

The next open house was slightly below average for the area and had not been upgraded. It was listed for $269,900 and had been on the market about a week.

Based on the "sold" data, Alex and JoLynn's home should be priced around $278,000 to $279,000 because they had updated the kitchen and replaced the carpets. However, it doesn't end there. They also need to factor in what other homes are on the market and what the local appreciation rate is.

Suppose this is a hot area, there are a few homes for sale and the local appreciation is running 2 percent per month, or about $5,000. Since the last comparable home sold about a month ago and another month would pass before closing if their home sold the first day or two, they should add at least $10,000 to their price. That would bring the estimated value up to about $289,000. If there are few homes for sale and the nicest home in the area is priced at $298,500 but no offers are made in two weeks, you know the upper limit. In this case, if you need a fast sale $289,900 would probably get it. If you want to play the market you could go $293,500, hope the competition sells in the next day or so, and you can be top dog and maybe squeeze another couple of thousand dollars out of the market.

As you can see, the upwardly moving target of a hot market makes pricing a home like rolling dice. How can you predict what a desperate home buyer will pay before prices go up another few thousand dollars by the next month?

It appears for a while that the usual appraisal and mortgage lending rules float in a space/time warp until eventually gravity again asserts control and the real estate market starts to regain some balance.

Pricing in a Stable or Declining Market

When the upward trajectory of a hot market starts to burn itself out and home prices start to slow down, an interesting market develops. Many home sellers refuse to believe the market is changing and cling to inflated expectations. Although homes may appraise for X dollars, it becomes more difficult to get that price due to increased competition.

Homes accumulate on the market as sellers who have to sell add to a growing and discounted inventory. This causes prices to slide; slowly at first, but as more homes come on the market the pace increases. This is the reason it takes longer for a slow market to develop than a hot market, which seems to ratchet up overnight.

So what do you do if you want to sell and you're in this type of market?

First, keep in mind that you want to attract home buyers who are looking for their dream home and are buying on emotion not hunting for bargains. The home and hearth buyers often pay closer to full price, but to attract this type of buyer you'll need to make your home as appealing as possible. (Upcoming chapters show you in detail how to do this and stay ahead of the competition.)

A good indicator of a slowing market is an increasing days on market (DOM) that multiple listing services track on every listing that sells. Average DOM stats are the pulse of an area's housing market.

When you use terms in your advertising like *discounted, best offer, moving must sell,* and so on all you do is attract price shoppers who make low offers. You'll net more money if instead you make your home more attractive and highlight it's desirable features in your ads.

Second, you'll need to be proactive and look at the homes currently for sale in your area, see how you stack up, and price your home accordingly. If there are several homes that are not as nice as yours, that's a plus. They'll help sell your home because agents and buyers will be comparing them to your home.

Third, rather than lower your price, offer a concession, such as paying the buyer's closing costs or throwing in the refrigerator or other appliances.

For example, when Wynn and Linda found themselves selling their home in this type of market, the first thing they did was tour the sixteen homes for sale in their area and price range. Five homes on the list hadn't been upgraded and still had the original paint and floor coverings. Three homes had been rentals and were not in good condition and four more weren't quite as bad, but still needed to be painted and have their carpets replaced.

The remaining four homes—priced $435,900 to $458,900—were the real competition: they had been upgraded with new paint, floor coverings, and had good curb appeal. In touring these homes, Wynn and Linda took a lot of notes on the advantages their home had as well as some of the disadvantages. Weighing their home's pros and cons, they decided to price their home at $248,900.

Here's how they sized up their home's pluses and minuses when compared with the competition:

- Linda was an artist and had used her sense of colors to highlight the architectural features of their home; namely, built-in bookcases, wainscoting, and molding. This would be the main selling feature they would highlight in their brochures, MLS photos, and ads, although it would not necessarily increase the home's value.

- Their home had hardwood flooring in the entryway, family room, and kitchen that tied the floor plan together and gave the home a more spacious look. The other homes they were competing against didn't have this flow. Again, something that would show well, but not add to value.

- The other homes had slightly larger lots, but not enough to seriously affect value. Not all homebuyers like to mow a lawn.

- Curb appeal was roughly equal, but Wynn and Linda's home had a couple of flower beds in which she had planted colorful annuals that complimented the yellow siding.

- They also did a lot of decluttering and rearranging to make their home look even more spacious. (How to do this is handled in a later chapter.)

As a result, Wynn and Linda's home sold for full price to the third couple who came through. Essentially, the home sold because of the great decorating that set it apart from the others and because of the time they spent to make the house more appealing to the buyer.

In another example, home sellers Ed and Christy decided to move to Arizona to be closer to her parents who had health problems. They called a part-time agent, Rhonda, whom Ed knew from work and asked her to come over and list their home.

The agent pulled up similar homes in the neighborhood that had sold. Her CMA compared the square footage, the year built, and the style of homes that sold in the last month or two.

The four homes that sold were priced in a tight group around $185,000, so that's what the agent suggested Ed and Christy list their home for.

The only problem was that the home was a dump. It badly needed

Before you list with an agent, make sure he or she has the showcasing skills to walk through your home with you and work up a list of problem areas. A friend or relative who is willing to be frank with you about your home's clutter and condition can also give you valuable input.

paint, floor coverings, and the rooms had too much furniture. Cat litter boxes needed to emptied bad and the kitchen was a disaster—it was hard to tell what color the counters were!

About ten agents took their clients through the first two weeks. They did a quick walk through and were out the door with few comments.

Soon word got around about the condition of the home and showings tapered off to zero by the end of the first month.

Another month went by with no showings and Ed and Christy started to feel the pressure; time was running out. They called their agent concerned that nothing had happened. Other homes in the area had long since sold and they were having no action. What did they need to do?

As is common with inexperienced agents, Rhonda had learned the fundamentals of putting together recent comparables to price a home, but hadn't developed the skills to factor in the home's condition. When a home doesn't sell and pressure builds, the only option many agents know is to lower the price. (Hey, lowering the price works for Wal-Mart!)

So the sellers lowered the price $10,000 to $175,000. Two weeks went by and still the home didn't sell, although one couple did look at it. Another week and another price reduction of $5,000 to $170,000. Finally, an investor looked at the home and offered $150,000 with a quick closing. Ed and Christy, by now pretty desperate, took it.

At closing, the sellers ended up taking a needless $40,000 loss. So in retrospect, what five things could they have done differently that wouldn't cost them so much equity?

1. They could have chosen an agent with experience and a track record as discussed earlier. The agent should have walked through with the sellers and written up a list of things to do before listing the home on the MLS.

2. Once agents active in the area saw the home, word spread that it was an overpriced dump and agents started to ignore it. Unfortunately, this is a common penalty for putting a home on the market too soon.

3. Soap and water are cheap. If the owners don't have time or don't want to clean the home, it's still much cheaper to hire a professional cleaning service than invite a lowball offer.

4. Decluttering is free and putting excess furniture, pictures, and knick-knacks into storage is inexpensive. (Decluttering is detailed in Chapter 2.)

5. Even if the sellers had to hire a painter, replace floor coverings, and use a cleaning service, the bill would be less than $12,000 for a home this size. That comes out roughly to $2.30 return for every $1.00 spent on presale preparation.

> In getting the most money possible from the sale, the condition of your home is what you have the greatest control over. If you ignore condition or *packaging*, as the marketing people call it, it'll come back to haunt you at the worst possible time.

The Five Components of Pricing a Home to Get the Most Money

These examples illustrate the importance of a home's condition, the fifth component of pricing, along with the location, the comparable sales, the competition, and the amenities.

It's almost a cliché to talk about how important location is in getting the most money when selling a home. But there's nothing you can really do to change your location unless you have a mobile home.

Other things you can't change in the selling game are the comparable sales in your area. This should make it evident that the condition of your neighbor's house plays a significant role in the value of your home.

The fourth important component is that competition boils down to the number of homes in your price range and area. If there are a few homes for sale, your price can go up; if there are many, your price will suffer. Economists call this supply and demand.

Amenities refer to what your neighborhood and area have to offer. If your house is located close to a transportation hub, medical center, school, or other desirable location, your price will go up. On many occasions, an older neighborhood's value will go up when redevelopment comes in or the proximity to a downtown makes the lots attractive for tearing down and rebuilding. But, in this case, you don't have much control.

So the biggest thing you have control over to get the most money possible is to focus on condition. And the rest of this book focuses on how you can take control and squeeze the dollars from your home so you can leave the closing with a big smile.

The next chapter, "Getting Your Home Ready To Sell" discusses a critical part of the sales process that too many sellers mess up on, leaving thousands of dollars for the buyer to scoop up.

CHAPTER 2

Take Control

Decluttering 101

The last chapter showed how appraisers and Realtors come up with the values they do and how they play the numbers game. But that's only part of the equation. Many people base their decision to buy homes more on emotion than on the numbers. When a certain home sparks a buyer's fond memories of hearth and home and fires off a bunch of emotional neurons, that's the home they buy. Numbers often enter the mix afterward to justify a decision they've already made on an emotional level. It then becomes a rush to write an offer before someone else beats them to their dream home. Price becomes secondary.

In the home selling game it's important to determine which sandbox you want play in. The first—sell your home "as is" and hope to get the best offer you can—has costly pitfalls. Namely, you end up selling by price, and that attracts bargain hunters who never pay full price for anything.

There are also more bullies in this sandbox, the kind who track homes that need a little work and have a high number of days on market (DOM). In other words, if, because of your home's condition, it sits on the market longer than others in the area do, the bullies will come looking for you. You will end up constantly fending off low offers, offbeat financing, excessive concessions, and sometimes out-right fraud. The bullies are interested only in the numbers and how good a deal they can get at your expense.

Playing in the other sandbox involves making your home as attractive as possible and pricing it based on the market. The skies here are a lot friendlier because you will be attracting the emotional buyers mentioned earlier and that translates into more money faster. In fact, you can expect between $2 to $10 return for every dollar you spend making your home more appealing.

Even more exciting for you is that few home sellers will go to the trouble of packaging their home so it shows at its best. (They think that playing in the first sandbox with the bullies will be more fun.) This spells opportunity because you can suck the wind out of your competitor's sails and get your home sold faster and for more money than they can.

But first, there are a few easy things you need to do to get your home ready to go on the market.

Step One: Look at Your Home as a Buyer Would

After you've lived in a home for a few years, it takes on the familiarity of a favorite sweat shirt where you don't notice the fading or worn places. Likewise, you're so used to your home that it's hard to see what would raise a buyer's eyebrow and cause them to lose all interest. You need to step outside this box of familiarity and look at your home as a buyer would; try to see what they will see when they come through the door.

For starters, walk across the street from your home with your digital camera (or camcorder) and a notepad. Take some pictures from down the street a short distance to about where someone driving to your home would first notice it. Then shoot a few shots from different angles walking up the street including a straight head-on photo.

Pretend, for a while, that you're a buyer driving up the street to your home. What's your first impression? (This is what the real estate people call curb appeal.) You may want to take a few digital shots to look at later as you complete your Curb Appeal Worksheet. Next, jot down a few notes on your worksheet to organize your impressions.

CURB APPEAL WORKSHEET

ITEM	CHANGES NEEDED
Curb and gutter need cleaning or replacing?	
Does the driveway need refinishing	
Shrubs need pruning or replacing?	
Trees need trimming or removal?	
Flower beds? Will planting annuals add color?	
Does walkway leading to the house need work?	
Fence need repair or painting?	
Lawn in good condition? Mowed and trimmed?	
Is your house number clearly visible?	
Are the steps and porch in good condition?	
Does the hand railing wobble or need refinishing?	
How about the entryway and front door?	
Are all the toys, tools, hoses, and anything else distracting put away?	

We all know how important first impressions are and how important the first few seconds are. It's almost a cliché, but nevertheless it's a reality we have to live with. That's why curb appeal is so important.

One seller found this out the hard way. He had a nice home in one of the better neighborhoods, but the front was obscured by fir trees, 18 inches in diameter, that he had planted too close together around a U-shaped driveway in front of the home.

The home should have sold the first week or two, but few people came through. Judging the home by the tangled forest in front of it, buyers would drive slowly by then go on to the next home on their list.

Although the real estate agent talked to the seller several times about the thicket of trees in the front yard, all he got was promises and no action. The seller continually put off tackling the job. Finally, out of exasperation the agent called the seller one Friday afternoon and told him he would be over early the next morning with his chain saw to help get the project jumpstarted.

For over two hours on Saturday morning, the neighbors endured the high-pitched whine of chain saws clear-cutting the front and side yard. When the saws were finally shut off, the results were remarkable. You could now see the house from the street and the rooms inside that faced the street were no longer dark, depressing rooms. And as a bonus, a buyer would get nearly a cord of firewood thrown in with the sale.

It took nearly a week for the seller to clean up the debris from the project, but it was certainly worth it. It didn't look like the same property and buyers started to come through. Less than two weeks later, a couple buying their first home made a full-price offer.

The clear message here is that if a home lacks curb appeal, it could languish on the market. Serious buyers—the ones you want to attract—see the days on market and wonder what's wrong with the house. If they go through the home with a what-is-wrong-with-this-dump attitude, your chances of getting a full-price offer are slim.

Another couple, Dan and Sondra, had an extreme case of not

First impressions are just as critical to selling your home as they are to your social life. Those first few seconds determine whether a buyer will come in and look, or drive on to the next home on their list.

being able to see their home as it really was. They built the colonial twenty years ago, raised their family in it, and had lots of good memories, but Sondra could no longer navigate the stairs so they decided to sell and look for a one-level townhouse.

The yard had taken on a wild look. Shrubs planted around the foundations had grown too tall and were too spread out. The lawns weren't bad, but needed trimming and fertilizer to bring them up to showing condition. And the asphalt driveway needed some minor repair and a coat of sealer.

The listing agent, Phil, was having a hard time getting these sellers to see their home as buyers would. The owners had lived there so long that they didn't want to change anything.

Finally, out of exasperation, the agent loaded the sellers into his car, drove them around the area, and pointed out several well-manicured homes. He even asked them to compare some photos he brought along of their home to the ones they drove by on the mini-tour.

On the way back, as they approached Dan and Sondra's street, Phil slowed down and told his clients to pretend they were buyers seeing their home for the first time. He asked them what their first impressions were? He also asked if they were shopping for a home, would they consider buying it?

As a result of their agent's patience and house tour, these sellers started to see the reality that their home needed some long-deferred maintenance and decided to take steps to put it into selling shape.

Unfortunately, many homeowners don't want to face the reality of their home's condition. Or they won't expend the effort and time to make their home salable for top price. These are the people who are more likely to get upset when low offers come in or their home sits on the market unsold.

Finally, here are three other things you can do to make clear the importance of seeing your home as a buyer would:

1. Visit new subdivisions and look at the model homes. Notice how they're decorated. The amount of furniture, the placement and number of pictures on the walls. Nothing is out of place; everything contributes to making the house feel like it's yours.

2. Tour open houses and homes for sale in your area, especially those that compete with your home. Look for negative features that the sellers haven't corrected. Notice what distracts you, what you like and what are big turn-offs.

3. Look at reality-based home shows on television and read a few decorating magazines. They may give you some good ideas you had not thought of.

Now that you know the importance of looking at your home as a buyer would and anticipating problems, the next step is critical to getting a buyer to emotionally warm up to your home.

It's Showdown Time: Stuff vs. Clutter

Whole books and articles tackle "decluttering" from a variety of approaches, such as spiritual, personality, organizational, and practical. Professional organizers even offer to make house calls for the overwhelmed. The real estate industry has also made it a buzzword and offers classes, but few agents know how to effectively counsel their sellers on how to declutter.

So what does this word mean that we hear so much about? Essentially, it means to get rid of all the stuff in your home that makes it look smaller and distracts a buyer. It's not about value, taste, or how much your possessions mean to you. It's about:

• Moving out excess furniture, which makes rooms look crowded and small, turning off buyers.

• Removing pictures, photos, trophies, and anything hung on walls that will distract buyers. You want them to imagine their stuff on the walls, right?

People buy homes based on dreams of how they would like to live, not their present reality. To sell for the most money you need to tap into those emotions.

- Creating an environment that gives buyers a feeling of home, where they could live happily ever after.
- Putting the odds in your favor so that you can generate multiple, full-price (or better) offers from buyers who compare your home to others on their list.

A home that's decluttered and packaged to sell has almost universal appeal. It's attractive to a high percentage of buyers whether they have great taste or no taste, good housekeeping skills or no housekeeping skills.

For example, one house-hunting couple who were not very good housekeepers or decorators (i.e., slobs) started out looking at homes that needed a little fixing up. Like so many other homebuyers, they heard stories of people buying homes and fixing them up for a big profit. They thought that would be a fun way to go for their next home.

After looking at several homes in need of work, these buyers decided that was not the way they wanted to go and began looking for a home they could move into without any work. The third home they saw pushed all their emotional buttons: they loved the colors with contrasting trim, the new floor coverings, and the spotless kitchen with granite countertops. It looked new, it smelled new. They couldn't live without it.

Even though the home was several thousand dollars more than they wanted to go, these buyers made a full-price offer and about a month later it closed—everyone was happy.

Unfortunately, fast-forward six months and you wouldn't recognize the home. It was no longer the spotless, beautifully decorated home the new buyers moved into. They created a slob heaven similar to what they had moved out of a few months earlier.

The flashing neon point this example makes is that even people who are slobs—from mild to hopeless—recognize a home's charm and make buying decisions similar to buyers who are more discriminating. This is why it's usually counterproductive to try to market your home without showcasing it first hoping to find buyers who don't care as much about the condition. They're out there but they're called investors—remember the sandbox bullies—and they buy only steeply discounted properties.

Decluttering for Dollars

Most decluttering magazine articles and books teach you how to organize and live with all your stuff. However, in this section decluttering takes on a different meaning: instead of living with it, your stuff takes a one-way route out of the house. Since you're going to move anyway, why not get an early start? You can box up and move a lot of your stuff into storage, schedule garage sales, or haul a few loads to a goodwill store without pressure.

Remove anything that will distract potential buyers from imagining themselves living in your home. You want to leave just enough furniture, pictures, and accessories to make the home look as if people live in it, so that buyers imagine themselves living in it.

Starting with the living room/family room, use the following worksheet to guide you:

LIVING ROOM/FAMILY ROOM DECLUTTERING WORKSHEET

ITEM	ACTION NEEDED
Furniture	Remove all furniture but a couch and loveseat, one or two lamp tables and an overstuffed chair or rocker. If it's a smaller room, leave only the love seat.
Pictures or Photos	Leave only one or two that will blend in with your décor. Even though you may have an extensive art collection you're proud of, your goal is to sell your home, not wow buyers who come through. Putting them in storage can be a good security move.
Carpets	Make sure your carpets are professionally cleaned and there are no spots or worn areas. Using plastic runners can keep traffic lanes clean. If carpets are badly worn, replace with a light, neutral color.
Hand railings	Railings are high profile. If they are made of wood and in good condition, wax may be all you need. If they are worn, sand and refinish, so they look like new. Metal can be spray-painted to look new.
Trophies	These are emotional items with many sellers. Yes, you did spend a lot of time, talent, and money getting them. But they're a big distraction with many buyers. The big trophy you caught in Baja may alienate a buyer who might otherwise make a full-price offer.
End Tables	One lamp and maybe one or two smaller items. No framed photos or large figurines. Groups of three items (rule of three) seem to resonate the best—that

	is, two chairs with an end table between them. Flower base and two small figurines on an end table and so on.
Mantels	Fireplace mantels are great collectors of distracting memorabilia. Clear them off, and depending on the material, clean them thoroughly and replace a few small items so you don't get a stark bare look.
Drapes/Blinds	Some sellers have drapes, sheers, and blinds. In many rooms, it's best to remove the drapes and sheers and leave only the blinds up. Clean the blinds and replace damaged parts. Heavy drapes often make a room look smaller and darker. The more light the better.
Potted Plants	If you have many potted plants, leave only a few that are in perfect condition and scaled to the room—that is, not too big. Absolutely no dead, dying, or wilted plants.
Curio Cabinets	If you have valuable crystal, figurines, antiques, or other collectables, pack them up and put them into secure storage or the garage. This not only removes a distraction, but also gives you some security in case thieves were posing as buyers.

After the living room is ready to be shown, next on the list is the kitchen. Many top agents feel this is the most important room in the house. And usually that's true: if the kitchen falls short of the buyer's expectations, it's out the door and on to the next home.

In one ten-year-old trilevel set in a good neighborhood, the seller's kitchen was so cluttered that it hindered the sale for over two months. The refrigerator was covered in magnets, bills, flyers, and yellowed newspaper clippings. A corner hutch bulged with incomplete china sets, knickknacks, and stacks of old magazines. Countertops were repositories for appliances, food wrappers, and even tools. Stacks of stuff were piled everywhere. Agents who showed it once, didn't make the same mistake twice.

Remarkably, the sellers refused to do anything about it. They couldn't or wouldn't see the obvious, that a home's condition had a direct influence on how it sells. The home languished on the market for three months before the sellers decided to move into another home across town that they received in an estate settlement.

It took the sellers six weeks to move all their stuff, and when it

A good Web site to locate hard-to-find replacement parts for range/ovens, refrigerators and other kitchen appliances is www.repairclinic.com

was finally vacant, the agent was able to talk the sellers into investing a few hundred dollars for a professional cleaning. To say it was a different house after it was cleaned would almost be an understatement. Agents in the area took new interest when the home went back on the market and, not surprisingly, the second couple who toured the home, bought it for full price. They loved the large, U-shaped kitchen and the spacious dining area.

In decluttering the kitchen, the following worksheet will keep you on track.

KITCHEN DECLUTTER WORKSHEET

ITEM	ACTION NEEDED
Eating/Dining Area	All hutches, curio cabinets, small tables, and other furniture in the eating area or nook have to go—leave the dining table only. You want this area to appear as big as possible.
Counters	This is a biggie: No coffee machines, appliances, cookbooks, or anything on the countertop. Not even crumbs from a breakfast muffin.
Refrigerator	All the magnets, calendars, original school artwork your kids created have to go. Leave nothing but a clean showroom surface.
Cupboards	Clean out all the cupboards and leave only what you need for day-to-day survival. Buyers open cupboards not only to be nosey, but also to see if their dishes and china will fit. Spilled Cheerios don't leave a good impression.
Cabinets Beneath Counter	Like the cupboards, clean out and leave only what you absolutely need. Be sure the sink beneath the cabinet is clean, with no leak stains, spilled cleaner stains, or other problems. Leave only a container or two of cleaner and dishwasher soap. If there's a musty smell, use a stick-on air freshener.
On Top of Cupboards	If your cupboards don't go all the way to the ceiling, it's likely this space has become a curio parking place. You guessed it: It all has to go.
Plants	Some homeowners like lots of plants in the kitchen, but too many create a clutter problem—two or three plants should be enough. If you're a plant collector, consider asking family or friends to plant sit while the home is on the market.
Dining Tables	Remove any extension leaves so the table takes up less space. Also, keep only the number of chairs you actually need. A large table with more than four chairs can make a dining space look smaller than it is. Also, putting a tasteful floral arrangement in the middle of the table does add a nice touch of color to the kitchen.
Pantry	Ah yes, for many homeowners the pantry is the repository of unfettered clutter. Since you're moving anyway, box it all up and move it out. It is

	fine to keep a few survival items, but nearly empty is best. Many buyers like to check out a pantry, so let them imagine their clutter on the shelves.
Drawers	Occasionally, buyers will check out drawers to see if there are dividers or organizers they like. Leave the fewest utensils you can survive with.

Bathrooms are next on the declutter list. Many buyers after looking at the kitchen turn their attention to bathrooms. These are important and you want to make sure nothing trips up your buyer's growing excitement as they progress through your home.

A word of caution: Remove all drugs from counters, medicine cabinets, and shelves and store them in another room out of sight. You don't know who is looking at your bathroom and sellers often lose prescription drugs to sticky-fingered lookers if the drugs are left accessible.

This next worksheet points the way to getting your bathrooms ready to show:

BATHROOM DECLUTTER WORKSHEET

ITEM	ACTION NEEDED
Countertops	Remove all personal items from the counters and make sure they're spotless.
Medicine Cabinets	Leave only minimum items in the medicine cabinet. Buyers usually don't peek in, but it happens.
Shelves	Leave no personal items on shelves, but replace with a couple of knickknacks that give the room a friendly look.
Under the Counter	Same as under the kitchen counter—everything must go. Use a scented stick-on to get rid of musty smells.
Tub/shower	Get rid of the soaps, shampoos, and everything else that is cluttering the shower nooks and tub rims. You want the bathroom to look like one you would expect to find in a five-star hotel.
Shower Curtain	Remove or replace it, especially if there's mold growing on it.
Towel Racks	One or two new towels only; more make the room look smaller.
Kitty Litter Boxes	This is a difficult one for cat lovers, but the litter box has to go somewhere out of sight. Many times buyers will enter the home, smell the litter box and make a U-turn out the door. Getting a friend or neighbor to take kitty when you're showing the home can help.

Typical buyers go through the front room to the kitchen, check out the bathrooms, and then go on to the bedrooms. This is where a buyer's excitement continues to build or collapses like a cheap tent in a heavy rain.

One common bedroom clutter problem sellers have is an over-sized bed with too much furniture. Buyers have rejected homes when they've glanced into the master bedroom, seen a king-sized bed with too much furniture, and concluded the room was too small. Later these same buyers ended up buying a home with the same size bedroom as the one they rejected. Perception is a powerful tool you ignore only at your peril.

So your potential sale doesn't stall out over the bedrooms, consider the following tips:

DECLUTTERING BEDROOMS

ITEM	ACTION NEEDED
Bed	Make sure the bed size fits the room. A wall-to-wall bed is a sure turnoff for most buyers. Store it and rent a smaller bed if possible.
End Tables	Put them into storage, if they crowd the room. Otherwise, remove everything off the top but a lamp and an alarm clock.
Dresser, Chest of Drawers, and so on.	Put them in storage, if they crowd the room. Also, clean everything off the top.
Armoires, Chests, and Wardrobes	All have to go into storage.
Chairs, Rockers, or other Furniture	Remove and store.
Bedspread and Pillows	Use a nice matching set that compliments the room's décor.
Drapes	This depends on the room size and décor. Most bedrooms with both drapes and blinds will look larger without the drapes.
Kids' Bedrooms	This is where having your home on the market will test your endurance. Yes, pick up the toys, dirty clothes and make the beds. These rooms do count with buyers too. You may want to box up all the toys but the few they play with daily.
Teenagers' Bedrooms	True, getting cooperation on keeping their bedroom showable can be like trying to climb a steep muddy slope. But the ceiling and wall posters need to go and the dirty clothes need to be picked up. Unfortunately, their room isn't an alternate universe where you can close the wormhole!
Closets	They're so important that a section devoted to closets is coming up.

After bedrooms, laundry rooms are important to many homebuyers. Although not often a sale killer, they can make a difference if it comes down to a dead heat.

When buyers come back for a second or third look, you can be sure they're trying to decide between your home and one or two others. This is when they really start zeroing in on things they glossed over the first time, and many times this is the laundry room.

Deciding which home to make an offer on when it comes down to two or more choices is highly stressful to buyers and their mindset shifts into elimination mode. They look for a reason to eliminate you from the playoffs. Don't make it easy for them to do so.

In one instance, a couple, moving due to a job transfer, narrowed their choices down to three homes and were having a hard time deciding on which home to make an offer. They had gone through all three homes twice and had to make a decision by 4:30 P.M. so they could catch their flight back to Chicago.

Stress levels were creeping up as the buyers and their agent poured over the listing printouts discussing the pros and cons of the three homes. One of the buyers remembered the laundry room in one of the homes was slightly larger than the other two, and since they had three kids, that could be a plus. They decided to go through the home again, since it was vacant and close by.

Although the laundry room was not significantly larger than the other homes, it appeared so with its new coat of light-colored paint and gleaming white tile floor. It also had a row of quality oak cupboards above the washer/dryer that matched those in the kitchen and the room was spotless.

The buyers looked at each other, nodded, and decided to go ahead and make an offer on this home. The agent wrote up the paperwork on the spot, the buyers signed it and left for the airport.

Was this laundry room substantially better than the ones in the other two homes? Not really. It was just enough better to get the buyers to come back for a third look and that tipped the sale.

Sometimes it's like the Olympics: A fraction of an inch or a tenth of a second determines the winner.

So you don't get zapped in a dead heat, consider these laundry room suggestions:

- Nothing should be on the counters or sitting on the appliances. No soap or fabric softener, containers or clothes.
- Move hampers, baskets, and other items to the garage or somewhere out of sight.
- Clean out cabinets in the laundry room. Buyers may take a peek.
- If you keep the kitty box in the laundry room, see the suggestions above in bathrooms.

Some home sellers feel they have a safe harbor for clutter in the closets. They often ask: "Do buyers really look in closets?" Absolutely! Your closets can make or break a sale. With some buyers, they're next in importance to the kitchen.

One home seller who needed a fast sale put his home on the market too soon. He refused to take the advice of his agent to get rid of the clutter, especially the overstuffed closets. Several qualified buyers looked at the home, but no offers were made. The home wasn't in the best condition and probably would have sold at a reasonable discount, in spite of the clutter, because of the area. It was the messy, stuffed closets that appeared to be the deciding turnoff for buyers.

With the pressure to sell building, the seller finally agreed to do something about the clutter. Cleaning out the double master bedroom closet and leaving only three or four items hanging in it, transformed it. The other two closets were more of a challenge; even cleaned out, they appeared small.

To counteract the space limitation of the two small closets, the seller installed closet organizers as well as the hall linen closet. He measured the closets, sketched rough layouts, and enlisted the help of a home improvement center nearby. The customer assistance person there helped the homeowner design the organizers, work up a list of materials, and figure the total cost. Because the seller wasn't too

Many buyers expect closets to have organizers. If your closets don't, check out home improvement centers. They have kits, design assistance, and some have carpenters they can recommend to do the install.

handy, he opted to hire a carpenter from a list the improvement center recommended.

A few days later, the carpenter installed the organizers and painted them a glossy white. The small dingy closets took on a new life. They no longer looked cramped and cluttered.

All told, the closet project cost the seller less than $2,000 and the home sold without the price concession of several thousand dollars the agent felt would be needed.

If your closets have that disorganized and cluttered look try the following:

- Of course, everything must go. Leave only a few must-have items hanging up or on shelves.
- Remove shoe holders and anything that clutters the closet floor.
- If your closets are dark and depressing, check out closet organizers at a home improvement center.
- Don't forget to shine or replace the closet doorknobs and other hardware.
- If you have bifolds or sliding closet doors, make sure they work perfectly and don't pop out of the track when opened. They should work smoothly and quietly.
- Remove anything on the back of the door: posters, mirrors, shoe holders, and so on.
- Replace inadequate light fixtures with new models that give off plenty of light.

Always assume that buyers will open the closets and look in. Storage is important and they want to know if their stuff will fit.

Garages

If the overflow from your closets ends up in the garage, this is when it catches up and corners you. You've run as far as you can run, you have to clean it out.

Garages are starting to come into their own with fancy car showroom floors, wall cabinets, lockers, and all sorts of accessories—about where kitchens were ten years ago. Dingy garages full of stuff won't cut it anymore; clutter can kill a sale deader than a CSI victim.

If your garage clutter pops that expectation bubble, buyers will drive to the next home without even a glance back through the rear-view mirror. So this doesn't happen to your sale, you may want to implement the following:

- If there's oil or other stains on the garage floor, use a degreaser, available at most hardware or car parts stores. When you're through degreasing, you may want to consider coating the floor with a sealant or epoxy coating to make it look sharp.
- Remove all the tacked on shelving, hooks, and similar hardware. Also, remove any workbenches you've installed. Important as they are, they give a garage a cluttered look.
- Take down the pegboards and box up all the tools and take them to storage.
- Patch holes and replace any damaged sheetrock especially those made by a car bumper.
- Paint the garage's walls and ceiling with a quality bright white paint.
- If your garage isn't finished (with sheetrock), you may want to hire a professional to sheetrock, mud, and tape it. This is especially important if other homes you're competing against have finished garages.
- Make sure the garage door and opener work flawlessly. Buyers will want to test how quiet it is for sure.
- Don't forget to wash the garage windows so they let in maximum light.

The Yard

By now, buyers touring your home should be getting pretty excited as they exit the garage to take a look around the yard. This is not the time to lose the big lead you've built up. Here are eight suggestions on decluttering your yard:

1. Make sure all tools, toys, bikes, garden hoses, and other items are picked up and stored in a shed or off-site storage.
2. Store extra vehicles, trailers, recreational vehicles, and so on off-site (unless you have a farm).
3. Take down the basketball standard attached to the front of the garage.
4. If its spring or fall, make sure the flower beds and garden are clear of dead vines and plants.
5. Prune shrubs and trees so they look neat and add to your curb appeal.
6. Remove all excess outdoor furniture off the porch, patio, and swimming pool areas. Leave no more than four chairs and a table to go along with the barbeque.
7. Hire a landscaping company, if needed, to make the grounds look good. More will be said on this in later chapters.
8. If you have a dog, a daily clean up program is important. You don't want a buyer stepping where Fido has gone to the bathroom.

Basements and attics are areas that often need decluttering. If these are finished into livable spaces, such as bedrooms or family rooms, declutter as you did in other rooms. On the other hand, if they are unfinished and used mainly for storage (clutter), now's the time to box the stuff up. You don't have to spend a lot of time on these storage areas, but keeping them neat in case a buyer takes a peek should do it. It's not often a deal killer.

If you're like most sellers who have arrived at this decluttered point, your home will feel a little bare and look a lot bigger. You may even feel uncomfortable with so many familiar things boxed up and moved to storage. But that's good, because you'll have less stuff to clean in getting your home ready to sell.

Tips on Storing Your Stuff

After a few years in a home, most people have accumulated a lot of furniture, sports equipment, yard tools, and so on. You can store it in the garage, but that would be counter-productive. You can impose on family or friends and fill up their garages or basements, but that could cost you a relationship. For most people, the best solution is to rent a storage unit for a couple of months. Here are a few tips to make hunting for a storage site easier:

- First, figure out how much square footage you need. Most storage units have eight- to ten-foot-high ceilings. Floor area in square feet is the length multiplied by the width. For example, a ten-foot-by-ten-foot unit is one hundred square feet.

- When you shop around, talk to movers who also have storage. The moving and storage industry is highly competitive and you may be able to negotiate a package deal and get a couple months of storage cheaper.

- Beware of movers who give you a price much lower than anyone else does. Ask around for referrals and note the companies that have been around for a while.

- Make sure you go with a month-to-month agreement. Rent is usually due on the first of the month and the first month is pro-rated. Ask about a discount if you prepay.

- Before you consider the storage company's insurance plan, check with your homeowner's insurance agent; a rider may be a lot cheaper way to go. But you do need to insure your storage unit's contents.

- Get a unit as close to your home as possible and one with access hours that fit your schedule.

With your home decluttered and in great showing condition, you probably won't need to think of long-term storage more than a few months. However, the temperature and humidity conditions of enclosed units are not stuff-friendly. The following precautions will help you prevent storage damage:

1. Use boxes that are uniform; they're easier to stack. Heavy boxes on the bottom, lighter on top.

2. Leave small walkways between boxes and furniture so you can easily get to items without moving boxes around.

3. Fill all boxes to the top. Use padding, crumpled newspaper, and so on. Half-filled boxes tend to collapse if anything is placed on them.

4. Wipe down metal objects—lawnmowers, file cabinets, tools—with a cloth sprayed with rust protector. Humidity can soar in an enclosed space.

5. Allow air to circulate by leaving a space between your stuff and the unit's walls and floor. Lay plastic sheeting on the floor or stack boxes on wooden pallets and use old sheets instead of plastic to cover items. If you live in an area prone to mold, ask the storage management what they recommend to prevent problems in your unit.

6. If your stuff can be damaged by humidity and temperature swings, consider shopping for climate-controlled storage. It's more expensive, but a lot cheaper than fixing damaged items.

With your home decluttered and having a leg up on moving, you will find it a lot easier to clean. The next chapter zeros in on cleaning tips that show your home at its best. It gives you lots of cleaning and money-saving shortcuts that will make your home irresistible to buyers coming through, especially if they've been looking at homes all day.

CHAPTER 3

Cleaning for Dollars

There are two ways you can clean a home: hire a professional cleaning company or do it yourself. Of course, hiring a professional leaves you free to have fun, while doing it yourself gives you dishpan hands but saves some bucks.

If the home will be vacant while it's on the market, spending a few hundred dollars for professional house cleaners just before you move is a money-making investment.

Sometimes homeowners are so frazzled by the time all their stuff is loaded that cleaning is usually done half-hearted or skipped entirely. That can adversely affect what they need most—a quick sale so they don't have to feed the mortgage interest alligator longer than necessary.

For example, one couple was so tired and eager to be on the road after they finished loading their 26-foot rental van, they skipped the cleaning and preparation work. Calling their agent on a cell phone, they told him where he could find a key to install a lockbox.

The sellers left the home in less-than-good showing condition: all the carpets had spots and desperately needed cleaning; it was obvious where pictures had been on the walls. In the kitchen, the empty refrigerator alcove had sticky stains on the floor that trapped a fuzzy collection of gray lint.

Although over a dozen buyers looked at the home that week, not one made an offer. A quick look and it was on to the next home on their list.

Finally, ninety days later, a buyer searching for fixer-uppers bought the home for close to what the sellers owed on their mortgage. After totaling up three months of payments, selling and closing costs, as well as lost equity, the sellers lost over $14,000 they shouldn't have.

If they would have spent $700 in cleaning, painting, and minor repairs, it would not have been a negative closing. In fact, every dollar they should have spent but didn't cost them $20 a few months later.

One broker solves these situations by working with a couple of cleaning companies that go in and clean vacant homes that owners have left in messy condition.

According to the broker, investing two to three hundred dollars in cleaning these listings almost always results in a sale, where otherwise they might languish on the market. For him, it's a smart business cost because he doesn't get paid until the home sells.

So whether you hire someone to clean your home or do it yourself, this chapter covers both alternatives. For the most part, however, it focuses on how to clean your own home from rafters to joists, so buyers wouldn't think of offering you anything but full price. It allows you to pull preapproved buyers from that nutrient-rich pool of those looking for their dream home.

Cleaning Your Home: Giving It That Wow Factor

The best time to clean your home is before you put it on the market. Many sellers wait until they list it or pound the "for sale" sign in the turf before thinking about getting it ready to show. As a result, cleaning often becomes hurried or half-hearted and it shows.

On the flip side, going the Mr. Clean route has its rewards. It's not uncommon for a home that's decluttered and clean to sell between the first and third preapproved buyer who looks at it in a normal market.

This can also save you some serious bucks. For example, if your mortgage payment along with taxes and insurance is $1,600 a month, that equates to over $53 a day. To recast this payment another way, every hour your home sits on the market unsold costs you $2.22, whether you're awake or asleep! Hopefully, this boosts your incentive to slip on those yellow rubber gloves.

In one case, when a woman who had a reputation as a near fanatical Mrs. Clean put her townhouse on the market, the neighborhood buzz brought her two offers the same day. Neighbors, seeing the sign go up, called their friends who were looking to buy and raved about the home's condition.

With this kind of word-of-mouth advertising, it would be difficult not to sell the home quickly and for full price.

Some interesting lessons learned from this are:

- Let the neighbors know you're planning on putting your home on the market.
- Let them know the steps you're taking to make the home attractive. If you're hiring a professional cleaning company, mention it.
- After it's clean and in showing condition, get as many neighbors through as possible, just before the sign goes up. Keep in mind the goal here is to let them see how clean and prepped the home is so they'll tell their friends and coworkers.
- Anything you can do to create an early buzz about your newly decluttered, clean home is a big plus.

The best time to start seriously cleaning your home is about a week before you put it on the market. A couple of hours each evening and a weekend should give you enough time to do a thorough job. It's important to have a plan of action or checklist that gives you a starting and ending point. A good how-to book on this is *Speed Cleaning 101* by Laura Dellutri, published by Meredith Books.

The following checklists will take you through the house and offer tips on how to solve stubborn cleaning problems, with an emphasis on areas that buyers commonly focus on as they walk through. As for the fix-it problems, they're covered in the next chapter.

Keeping your home clean or keeping sections clean as you do them can be a challenge. You can save yourself work and eliminate 80 percent of the dirt coming into your home by following what many

Cleaning Info Websites

www.healthyhousekeeper.com

www.surfaceshields.com

www.surfacedoctor.com

www.repairclinic.com

www.pioneerthinking.com/cleaningsolutions.html

www.allabouthome.com

www.familydigest.com

builders do at home shows: have a "no shoes in house" rule. A small rug just inside the door for family or friends and later on for buyers to leave their shoes on works great.

Or, as an alternative, get a box of disposable shoe covers available at most paint stores. Buyers can slip these over their street shoes and not feel uncomfortable walking around in mismatched or holey socks.

Along with the shoe covers, you may also want to consider getting a roll or two of self-adhering protective film (see www.surfaceshields .com) that protects newly cleaned carpeting. This is especially a good way to go if you hold an open house and a lot of people come through. This not only contains the dirt but sends a strong message to buyers that this is a clean, well-cared-for, above-average home worth more than other homes they've looked at.

It can be interesting to check out competing sellers in your area and see if they're requiring buyers to remove their shoes or offering shoe covers. If you're the only one, use it as a marketing tool. Let buyers know you offer a home that's cleaner and in better condition than the competition.

So, with resolve firmly in place and gloves on, start with the entryway. The following checklist points the way to create a good first impression:

ENTRYWAY AND LIVING ROOM CLEANING CHECKLIST

ITEM	CLEANING SUGGESTIONS
	CAUTION: Always read the labels; mixing cleaners can be deadly.
Door	Clean the door with any good grease-cutting spray cleaner. Use a metal-polishing cloth to shine the metal hinges and doorknob. If re-finishing is needed, the next chapter will cover the how to.

(continues)

Entryway	If you have carpet, put an attractive mat in the entryway after you've cleaned the carpets. For tile, clean the grout with peroxide or four parts water to one part bleach. Apply grout white that comes in a paste to restore the grout, then be sure to seal the grout with a sealer available at home centers. Hardwood floors can sometimes be shined up with a restore cleaner. If that doesn't work, consider refinishing the floor.
Flooring	It's best to use a professional carpet cleaner that can take out the tough spots and add a deodorizing solution. If this isn't an option, rent a carpet cleaner and follow the directions on the cleaning chemicals that come with it. For hardwood floors that are beyond cleaning but not too damaged, you can recoat with polyurethane. Check a home center for products and tools. There are also professionals who can sand and recoat the floor to new condition. Get two or three bids before you commit if you go this route.
Woodwork	A great treatment for wood is lemon oil. You may have to shop around to find the real thing. Read the label before you buy. Use to cover scratches and restore luster on all wood surfaces. The components of a stairway—wood or metal balusters, balustrades, and railings—are high-profile items, as are chair rails. If surfaces are worn you should sand, stain, and recoat with varnish or polyurethane. A quality spray paint works well for metal.
Walls	If you have a formal entryway, make sure the walls, baseboards, and other molding are in perfect condition. No scuff marks, dirt, or dings here. If needed, refinish or paint.
Lighting	This is high profile. If your light fixtures don't add to your home's décor, consider replacing them. Clean all fixtures and replace burned out bulbs so they all have equal wattage.
Windows	Windows should be spotless. The woodwork around entryway windows should be clean and in good condition. If you have both blinds and drapes, remove the drapes and store—leave only the blinds up.
Wood trim: baseboards, window, and door trim	Make sure all trim is in good condition: wipe down with a damp microfiber cloth. If the finish is scratched, dented, or worn it should be sanded and stained or painted.
Odors	Bad odors can kill a sale quicker than anything can. For pet accidents in carpets and mold on tile grout, use an enzyme cleaner. Inject the cleaner into the carpet pad with a syringe on bad-smelling areas before you clean the carpets. If odors come from kitty litter, move it outside or into the garage. Have a friend drop by and do a nose test in case you're accustomed to a few resident smells.

From the entryway, buyers usually head through or past the living room with anticipation for what the kitchen is like. If they like what they've experienced so far, they're hovering around a 5.5 on a 10-point buying scale. The kitchen can ratchet the score up substantially or kill a budding decision; it's that important. The following kitchen checklist makes sure your score goes up substantially.

KITCHEN CLEANING CHECKLIST

ITEM	CLEANING SUGGESTIONS
Floors	This is a biggie. Clean with damp microfiber mop to eliminate any accumulated soap buildup. If the floor is still dull, use a vinyl floor restorer or polymer product. If these don't kick some life into the floor, you'll need to replace it. Tile floors often mean cleaning the grout, applying grout white, and resealing.
Counters	Buyers zero in on counters so they should be in perfect condition. For laminate that's not worn too badly, you may be able use a restorer. Check the yellow pages under countertops for laminate restoration professionals. If beyond help, replace. With tile counters, clean and make sure grout is resealed. Other types of counter materials should be cleaned and in excellent condition.
Cabinets	Cabinets need to be cleaned and treated with lemon oil or the equivalent for a great shine. If your cabinets have seen better days, Chapter 4 outlines several refinishing options. And yes, buyers will look inside, so don't skip this step.
Pantry	Should be decluttered, cleaned, and painted a gloss white if needed.
Hood/Exhaust Fan	Clean and degrease under the hood. Replace the filter if it has one and make sure the lights and fan are working. If the unit has seen better days, replace.
Stove	Many buyers will open the oven and look in, so it should be spotless. Even though you may have an automatic cleaning oven, give the inside a quick cleaning with an all-purpose or window cleaner to give it a shine. Make sure all elements work and knobs are new looking. For replacement elements and knobs, go to www.repairclinic.com or look in the yellow pages under appliance repair. Of course, the stove top should be image-reflecting clean.
Dishwasher	If your dishwasher is older or not in top condition, replace it with a middle-of-the-line model. Leaks, rust spots on the racks, and a stained liner do not give a good impression. It should be empty and smell good for any showings.
Refrigerator	As mentioned in the previous chapter, nothing but a clutter-free, clean surface. The inside should be neat and smell good, especially if you're including it in the sale.
Light Fixtures	Light fixtures should be cleaned and in good condition. Replace bulbs with as high a wattage as you can safely use. If you've used 60-watt bulbs, try going to 75 or 100. The more light in the kitchen the better.

(continues)

Windows	Clean windows inside and out. If you have curtains that add to your kitchen's charm, leave them up. Otherwise, leave just the blinds.
Table	Of course, the table should be clean and attractive. A later chapter will give suggestions on how to showcase the table and kitchen.
Odors	To give your disposal a great smell, run a cut-up lemon through it. Counter to what the ad people on television say, it's not a good idea to burn candles in a house. The smoke collects on the ceiling and leaves an oily deposit; you'll find out where, the next time you paint the room. Instead, get a small hot plate that heats the candles and releases the scent without a flame. If you use scent dispensers, go sparingly and use the same flavor throughout the house. The kitchen garbage can be an unpleasant odor source, so use disposable liners to eliminate frequent cleaning.
Sink	The sink should be spotless with no hard water spots, rust stains, or damage. Use vinegar to get rid of water spots and a light coating of mineral oil to give stainless steel sinks a shine.
Faucets	Faucets should be in perfect condition. Absolutely no drips. Replace them if worn or damaged. Shine metal parts with window cleaner.

From the curb to the kitchen, the buyer's excitement should steadily grow as they explore the home. Because the kitchen is usually the home's focal point, they'll often linger there savoring the effects you've created with your hard work: checking out the cupboards, pantry, and appliances. Sure, they'll move on to the rest of the home, and if there are no surprises, a buying decision starts to gel.

From there, the excitement of finding their dream home kicks in as buyers give their agent a smile, a nod, or mouth the words, "This is it!" Are they thinking of writing a low offer at this point? No way. Their thoughts are on making an offer fast so someone else doesn't beat them to their dream home. And that offer is usually full price with as few contingencies as possible.

One home that was exceptionally clean and showed great had four nearly identical full-price offers at the same time. The sellers had the enviable task of picking which offer they wanted, and not having to counter to get the best price. None of these buyers wrote a low offer because their focus was on getting the home not a good deal.

If your home doesn't wow the buyer, there's usually no heat-of-the-moment excitement, leaving home shoppers to focus on value and condition. The emotion of, "This is my dream home!" is replaced by a pillager's lust for a good deal.

Of course, excited buyers are still going to look at the rest of the home before fumbling for a pen to write an offer, and that puts bathrooms next on the cleaning list:

BATHROOM CLEANING CHECKLIST

ITEM	CLEANING SOLUTION
Floors	If the floor is tile, it's back to grout cleaning and sealing. Vinyl should be cleaned or replaced if glue has failed and it's starting to curl.
Walls	Walls should be as clean as an operating room. If you have wallpaper that is peeling, wild, dark, heavy-patterned, or psychedelic, it's best to strip it off—wallpaper strippers are available at home centers—and paint the room a light neutral (read: white) color.
Fixtures	These should be clean and shiny. Faucets that leak should be fixed or replaced especially if the chrome finish is damaged. Don't forget doorknobs, pulls, and hinges.
Mirrors	Glass cleaner and a microfiber cloth leave a streak-free shine. Mirrors that are damaged should be replaced.
Sink	Many bathroom cleaning products do a good job on porcelain sinks. It's important to remove all rust and hard water stains. If the sink is chipped, replace it or try using the repair kits available at hardware stores. This can also work for chipped tubs.
Shower/Tub	This is a bathroom biggie. Clean the tile and make sure the grout is clean and sealed. For other surfaces, use a manufacturer-recommended cleaner. Recaulk where tile or some other surface meets the shower pan. Shower doors need to be cleaned with a hard water remover so the metal is shiny and new looking. Absolutely no hint of mold or water damage should remain. Replace shower curtain and hangers. If necessary, recaulk around the tub.
Cabinets	Use lemon oil to shine cabinets. Replace if damaged. Inside, the bottom of the cabinet should be clean and not have any water damage. Make sure there's no mold or bad smells. Clean and shine the plumbing U-trap, and lines. Check for corrosion and leaks on the turn-off valves while you're cleaning under the sink.
Head (toilet)	Whatever you want to call it, it should be spotless with no bowl water stains. Any grocery store or home center has several brands of toilet cleaners that do a good job. Replace the seat and hardware if needed. If the porcelain is cracked or damaged, replace the unit.
Lights	Make sure the light fixtures above the sink are clean and polished. Multibulb fixtures should have the same wattage bulbs. Kick up the bulb wattage a notch if you can safely. Don't forget to clean the switch covers, replace if old or cracked.

Light, bright, and spotlessly clean bathrooms may be boring, but they give buyers a clean canvas to indulge their decorating fantasies. Let them peek in, see all is acceptable, and move on to inspect other rooms.

After getting the bathroom in showing condition, you'll probably start wondering if all this is worth it. To keep you motivated, remember the better a home looks, the quicker it sells and the sooner all of this will be over. Oh, and you'll have more money to spend on your next home.

As mentioned in Chapter 2 on decluttering, you absolutely don't want bedrooms looking smaller than they really are. If you followed through on moving out everything but the bare necessities, cleaning should be a snap.

If you have teenagers, you'll undoubtedly face a few extra challenges cleaning their rooms. You might try the argument that since you're moving shortly, they can get a head start by removing and packing the posters stuck to the walls and ceiling. If they've painted the room purple, black, or psychedelic red, you'll need to repair the damaged walls and upgrade the room to a more earthly white. A few scent-dispensing plug-ins won't hurt either.

Buyers can be understanding, especially if they also have teenagers, but don't count on it. They're still comparing your home's bedrooms to others on their list.

Here are a few suggestions to make bedrooms standout:

- All woodwork should be cleaned and shined with lemon oil or equivalent.
- Walls should be cleaned or repainted a light color.
- Windows should be sparkling clean and drapes cleaned or removed.
- Carpets should be cleaned and adhesive-backed plastic—available at paint stores—laid over the traffic areas. Hardwood floors need to be clean or refinished.
- Ceiling fans and light fixtures need to be cleaned and bulbs replaced; go to a higher wattage if possible.

An important part of bedrooms are the closets. Some older homes have teensy ones that hold two coats and a hat, so it's critical to have these almost empty and clean. If needed, paint walls and ceiling with a gloss white paint. You want to encourage every light ray possible to ricochet around in these closets. Of course, closet doors should be clean and their hardware shined or replaced.

Organizers sometimes make small closets look more appealing and the next chapter covers how to do this.

At this point, buyers looking at your home should have covered the main levels. If your home is a rambler (ranch) and has a basement, serious buyers will want to check that out next.

Finished basements with bedrooms, baths, and a family room are part of the living space and should be delcuttered and cleaned the same as the upstairs.

If the basement is unfinished, you still need to make it look spiffy. Make sure there are no spider webs, water stains, or other distractions.

Attics are treated the same as finished or unfinished basements. Yes, this is going the extra mile, but you want to keep the wow factor going because most of the competition won't do all this. When it comes time to write an offer, what home do you think buyers are going to be raving about?

Cleaning the Exterior

Your home's exterior is an important component of curb appeal; fortunately it's not difficult to make your home look new again. The easiest and safest way is to rent a high-pressure cleaner from an equipment rental company. You can clean the house's exterior, driveways, walkways, porches, foundations, fences, patios, and so on in one project.

Pressure cleaners can be either gas or electric powered and deliver a jet of water at 1400 pounds per square foot through a trigger-controlled wand. You can add detergent to the water for even more efficient cleaning. Attachments and extensions make it possible to clean the exterior of your house without a tall ladder. Also exciting, pressure cleaners do a great job removing driveway oil stains from your car restoration site and years of accumulated grime from other surfaces.

Here are some tips for renting and using a pressure cleaner:

• Call several equipment renters for cost and minimum times. Some have two- to four-hour minimum times. The average house, driveway, and walks shouldn't take more than four hours.

- Make sure the machine you rent has a detergent-adding attachment. Most manufacturers suggest a mix of water to normal household detergent of twenty to one.
- If you have painted siding, test clean a small spot to make sure the pressure setting doesn't abrade the paint job.
- Also, test a small area on aluminum or vinyl siding to make sure your setting will not cause damage.
- Start at the bottom and work upward so the detergent-water mix won't run down and cause streaking.
- Rinse sprayed surfaces off thoroughly with clean water.

Unfortunately, pressure cleaners don't do a good job on windows, and no home showcasing project is complete without squeaky-clean glass. This brightens the home's interior and causes sharp images to reflect off the windows outside. Buyers walking up to the house can't help but notice with a touch of awe.

The following window-cleaning technique isn't the only way to clean windows, but it's similar to the way many professional windows cleaners go about their craft. With a squeegee, scrubber, bucket, lint-free cloths (microfiber cloth works great), extension pole for second story windows, and a little detergent, you're ready to go.

The following steps show how the pros do it:

1. Use a lamb's wool or cloth-strip applicator with a telescoping pole.
2. Fill a five-gallon bucket with warm water and a short squirt of dishwashing detergent.
3. Load up the applicator with cleaning solution and scrub down the window.
4. Starting at the top, pull the squeegee over the pane going from right to left (or left to right if you're one of the 16 percent of the population that's left-handed). When you get to the end of the stroke, wipe the squeegee's blade with a microfiber cloth. Continue with the squeegee stokes until you get to the bottom.
5. Remove any water left on the glass edges with another microfiber or chamois cloth.
6. Don't wash windows when direct sunlight is hitting the glass. The sun will dry the soap solution and make it impossible for you to squeegee it off.

Window Cleaning Supplies

Ettore squeegees: www.ettore.com

Zud cleaner: www.doityourself.com

Barkeeper's Friend: www.barkeepersfriend.com

Cleaning supplies: www.keysan.com

Cleaning supplies: www.windows101.com

For mullioned windows (windows with small panes), you may need to use a smaller applicator, like natural sponges or bristle brushes, that lets you get into the corners.

You'll also need a smaller squeegee that fits the panes. If you can't find one, try cutting a larger squeegee down with a hacksaw to fit. Leave the rubber part about one-quarter inch longer on each side of the resized metal holder.

After scrubbing down the pane, squeegee from top to bottom and wipe off the rubber strip after each stroke as you do with larger windows.

If you have hard water stains, try using Zud or Barkeeper's Friend, a cleansing powder that contains oxalic acid. Mix the powder into a paste, scrub down the window, and then clean and squeegee as you did on the other windows.

That's all there's to it. No gallons of window cleaner and rolls of paper towels. But if you don't want to do all of this yourself, there's another route that frees you up for a round of golf or two and the buyers won't know.

Hiring a Cleaning Service

You can go several ways in hiring someone to clean your home, namely:

1. Go with a national franchise service.
2. Look for a local company that has a good reputation.
3. Hire a newer company that maybe will give you a better deal.
4. Go with a referral from someone you know.
5. Hire someone off the street on the cheap.

Regardless of which way you go, here are some important considerations you may want to make in your hiring decision:

- Whomever you hire should be bonded, insured, and licensed if required in your area. Bonded means that if a worker damages something in your home, there's a third party to make it right. Hiring insured workers are important in case they get injured cleaning your house. You don't want to turn a cleaning job into a lawsuit. If the people you hire are not insured, contact your homeowners insurance provider and add a rider if needed. Always ask for proof of in-force insurance coverage up front before anyone starts work.

- If it's someone you don't know, talk to a couple of their past customers.

- Secure all prescription drugs and valuables in a locked cabinet or closet. You'll also want to do this when you show the home or hold an open house.

- Get a firm bid in writing up front, listing what cleaning is included and the final price.

- Make sure you get a written guarantee and do a quick walk through before you write that check.

National franchises can be a good way to go because their employees are professionally trained, bonded, and insured. Like the burger people at the golden arches, their quality control is usually consistent.

Cleaning Service Websites

www.house-cleaning-services.com

www.merrymaids.com

www.maids.com

www.maidpro.com

www.servicemagic.com

www.hire-a-maid.com

www.dexonline.com (yellow pages)

Although costs will vary depending on where you live, a typical home costs from $250 to $350 and takes anywhere from three to five hours. A home that's really bad—perhaps shelters a goat or two—may cost up to $500 plus.

Local cleaning companies can also give you good service. Check out the yellow pages under house cleaning and you should find a sizable list of vendors.

To avoid surprises, it's best to have a representative look at your home and give you a written bid to compare with one that gives you prices over the phone.

Hiring someone off the street to do the job on the cheap is another option. If you go this route, make sure your homeowners insurance covers a 911 call if the cleaner falls off a ladder.

One homeowner trying to save a few bucks had this happen when she hired someone recommended by a neighbor. In the fall, the cleaning lady broke her arm in two places, requiring surgery and a couple of days in recovery.

Unfortunately, the homeowners insurance wouldn't cover the accident and the sellers ended up liable for thousands of dollars in medical costs.

In the process of cleaning, decluttering, and adding the wow factor to your home, you probably found a few things that needed repairs or upgrading. The next chapter shows you how to decide what to fix, what to replace, and what to upgrade so you don't waste any of the hard-earned equity your cleaning efforts are building.

CHAPTER 4

Repairs/Upgrades That Make or Cost You Money

As you went through your home cleaning and decluttering, undoubtedly a few items caught your attention that needed fixing or replacing. At this point, many home sellers wonder what they should fix and what they should replace. Of course, the thought also creeps in that the more money you spend the less you walk away with at closing.

This chapter tackles that economic reality head on with specific suggestions on what to replace and what not to. And of equal importance, how to avoid potential deal killers upfront so the sale goes smoothly.

One home seller forgot economic reality when he reshingled his roof before putting the home on the market. While completing the job, he got to thinking how great new siding would look and had the contractor do that as well. In total, he spent close to $20,000 for the project.

Later, when the appraisal came back, the upgrades had increased the value less than $2,500. The seller was understandably upset, but the appraiser explained to him that buyers expect a nonleaky roof and siding in good condition—they're not extras.

In this case, the owner should have replaced the roof only. The siding was in good shape and the owner's reason for replacing it was personal taste rather than its condition.

This often happens when you confuse repairs with upgrades. It's important to know the difference so you don't lose money when getting your home ready to sell.

Repairs refer to those items you need to fix or replace in order to sell, pass an appraisal or inspection. While they don't add much to the sales price, without them the sale may not happen at all. They often pop up a few days before closing and create a tense situation that takes the fun out of selling if you haven't done your homework.

On the flip side, upgrades are trickier: they're items you fix up or replace to make the home more saleable. If you do too much, you lose money; too little, you don't get the desired effect from the time and money invested.

How to know what to fix and what to upgrade is the focus of this chapter. You'll learn step-by-step how to eliminate the guesswork.

Sometimes sellers ask why they should spend money on an upgrade only to increase the home's value by the same amount or less. If that's all an upgrade returns, you likely wouldn't spend money doing it. But in reality, you end up with important benefits, namely:

- Improvements often make the home sell faster; you save on mortgage interest, property taxes, insurance costs, and other fees. Plus, when it sits on the market unsold for a few weeks, you start attracting bargain hunters and investors who make steeply discounted offers.

- Appealing homes attract emotional buyers who are less likely to give you a lowball offer.

- The whole is often greater than its parts. Repairs and upgrades can make a house more desirable than the competition. That means you can price it a little higher and end up netting more money.

Of course, the key is to know what and how much to upgrade or repair so you don't lose money.

How to Identify Needed Repairs

Alan and Maria had lived in their '54 bungalow for about eight years when they stopped by a new subdivision across town. One model they toured ignited their imagination. It was their dream home and they couldn't live without it. But first, they would need to sell their current home.

Although they hadn't made many upgrades to their bungalow, everything appeared to be in good working order for a fifty-two-year-old home, they reasoned.

Maria called a friend who sold real estate and asked her to come over. The agent did a quick walk-through and went over some comparable properties that recently sold in the area. According to recent sales data, the home should sell for about $230,000, the agent told an excited Alan and Maria who had bought the home for $115,000. After paying off their $91,700 mortgage and selling costs, they would net about $122,500, close to the down payment it would take to buy their new dream home.

After listing their home for $234,900, they contacted the builder, signed a purchase contract, and put down a $12,000 deposit. They had three months to get their home sold and closed; it was a tight schedule that didn't leave much wiggle room.

Several buyers came through the first couple of weeks, but none made an offer. Then, at the end of the fourth week on the market, an older couple made an offer. It was low and the sellers countered back

Give yourself 30 to 60 days to put your home in selling shape before you put it on the market. This gives you time to track down replacement parts, plan upgrades, and take care of problems. You don't want surprises during the stressful time you're showing your home or after you get an offer.

at $230,000. After two more counters over the next three days, the sellers finally agreed on $225,000 because time was running out.

The real estate purchase agreement had a provision that made the offer subject to a professional home inspection and appraisal. The buyer's agent had written in a twenty-one-day deadline for both. As he explained, the buyers didn't want to invest several hundred dollars until they were sure the lender would approve them for the loan. Unfortunately, the listing agent and Alan and Maria didn't take this seriously, and the buyers took two weeks to schedule a home inspection.

Two days after the inspection the buyer's agent faxed the listing agent an addendum detailing a list of problems the inspector found. They wanted the items fixed or replaced before they would proceed with the sale. That gave Alan and Maria about a week to do the work or lose the sale and end up back at square one.

Many of the repair items were minor such as missing switch covers in the basement, spliced wiring that wasn't in an electrical box, and blocked attic vents. However, two major problems were a cracked combustion chamber in the gas furnace and a leaking water heater. The cracked chamber allowed carbon monoxide to escape when the furnace fired up—a potentially lethal problem. The leaking ten-year-old water heater obviously needed replacement.

Unfortunately, the sellers couldn't get a heating contractor to replace the furnace and water heater for two weeks. That left two alternatives, extend the closing by at least a week or offer to escrow funds and let the buyers handle it.

Neither alternative worked. The buyers, spooked by the home inspector's report, opted to back out of the sale. This left the sellers in a tense situation. They had less than a month to find another buyer and close so they could meet the contract deadline on their new home.

Consider hiring a professional home inspector before you put an older home on the market. You don't want deal-killing repair problems popping up. Look for home inspectors in the yellow pages under *Home & Building Inspection* or go to: www.ashi.org and www.nahi.org

Fortunately, the builder agreed to an extension, but Alan and Maria lost the interest lock on their loan. This ended up costing them one-half of a percent more when they renewed their loan commitment a month later. Plus, they discounted their home another $5,000 to get a fast sale on top of $4,600 to replace the furnace and water heater. They were not happy home sellers.

With the clarity of hindsight, what could Alan and Maria have done differently?

1. Much blame should go to the agent. She not only failed to consider the condition of the home, but also failed to notice that other homes in the area at that price range had newer furnaces and water heaters. Many also had done extensive remodeling and upgrades.

   In other words, the agent failed to factor in the home's condition when she priced it. This stretched the selling time resulting in a $15,000 discount. Also, the agent didn't walk through the home and make a list of repairs and upgrades the home needed to be competitive.

2. The homeowners should have hired a professional home inspector to find out if there were serious problems before listing the home. This is something homeowners should always do on a home that is fifteen years old or older.

3. When the offer came, the agent should have called the buyer's lender and verified the preapproval data. If accurate, this should raise a flag about why the inspection and appraisal deadlines were three weeks away instead of ten days or less. You want to keep a short leash on these deadlines, because you end up taking your home off the market longer than necessary.

Incidentally, you should never accept an offer unless the buyers have a letter from the lender stating they've been preapproved. Even then, you should follow up and verify the approval. In fact, according to *Inside Mortgage Finance,* a trade magazine published by Campbell Communications, preapproval letters from almost 40 percent of Internet-based lenders, 30 percent from mortgage brokers, and 20 percent from national lenders are faulty. Translation: Loan officers sometimes lie or omit that there are unresolved credit or income problems when they give buyers preapproval letters. Sometimes the problems are worked out in the days between offer and closing; other times they aren't and the deal goes south.

When buyers go through a home and find problems, their thinking goes into what-else-is-wrong-with-this-dump mode. From there, it's down hill and you lose all chances for a good offer. Even concessions to fix problems often fail to work because the buyer's confidence has evaporated.

Some sellers feel they can offer a repair concession up front, so they don't have to take care of problems. This usually backfires because the people who make good offers are looking for a home to live in problem free. Those who are willing to buy a home with problems commonly discount the house heavily and ask for concessions too. It becomes a no-win for the seller. A much better strategy is to fix the problems and price the home at market value.

Another common mistake sellers often make is offering a decorating allowance. They reason that letting the buyer pick out their colors will create a marketing edge.

But this doesn't always work out. As previously discussed, you want to attract buyers who are looking for their dream home because they pay top price. These buyers often don't want to pick out floor coverings, paint colors, or other items; they want to close as quickly as possible and move in hassle free.

As Judy Morrill, a Utah home renovator with thirty years of experience, puts it: "When we renovate a home and put in new flooring, new paint, and other items, we stay with light neutral colors that pretty much go with any furniture. Our homes always sell fast and for nearly full price. We try to reduce it to what you see, is what you get."

If you're not the handy type, ask around and find a handy man who will come in and take care of your fix-it list. Before you start, write up a simple agreement that outlines the hourly payment, the list of items to be fixed, and the timeframe. In other words, put it all in writing.

Fix-It Checklists to Keep You on Track

To help you track down problems that can surface and ruin your sale, check out the following fix-it lists:

FIX-IT CHECKLIST

ITEM	SUGGESTED ACTION
Entryway	If the door won't clean, sand it down with 220-grit sandpaper and restain or paint. Painting the door a contrasting color to the siding creates an interesting entryway. Intense shades of red, burgundy, blue, green, and purple—gloss or semigloss—are popular door colors that work well. As for the storm door, it depends on what's needed in your area. It should be in new condition with a good seal.
Door Hardware	These should look new and shiny. If they don't, replace because these are high-visibility items.
Entryway Floor	If the carpet is worn and due for replacement, you may want to create a tile, laminate, or other entryway three or four feet into the room. This looks good and saves new carpet from front-of-door wear.
Wall Behind Door	A common repair problem occurs where the doorknob punches a hole in the wall. There are several types of impact-absorbing covers you can apply over the hole, if it's not too big. If you plan to paint the wall, go to www.home repair.about.com/od/walls/a/fix_holes.htm for a great site on patching sheetrock holes.
Floors	Wood floors need to be in like-new condition. You can sand and restore them yourself or hire a professional. If it has been a few years and the floor is in bad condition it's probably best to let a pro handle it. A good wood floor website is www.doityourself.com/woodfloors.
	Carpets that won't clean to new condition should be replaced. Go with a light, neutral color. Midgrade acrylic fiber carpet gives you the most bang for the buck. Also, replace carpet padding with midgrade quality.
	Vinyl that has lost its shine also needs to be replaced. Go with a midgrade quality. Avoid textured or patterned vinyl that traps dirt and is hard to clean.
Fixtures	Repair broken or loose light fixtures. Glass parts can usually be found at home improvement centers. Replace a light fixture if it doesn't put out enough light or doesn't fit the décor. Ceiling fans should be working and blades in good condition. Replace pull chains if broken or in bad condition.
Faucets	If the chrome is worn, you'll need to replace. Usually a good cleaning with an old toothbrush and hard water build-up remover works. Faucets that drip need new washer or cartridges replaced. Check out www.plumbing.hard warestore.com/learning/how-to-repairfaucets.aspx this is a great how-to website. Take your old parts to a plumbing supply store for replacements. Attach an aerator to your faucet if it doesn't have one. You don't want water to splash all over when a buyer turns on the tap.
Appliances	It's important that kitchen appliances have matching colors. If you're going to replace them, definitely go with matching colors. Appliances that are in

good condition but don't match can be professionally refinished to match and save some bucks. Check out the yellow pages under *Appliances—Refinishing.*

Cabinets	Kitchen, bathroom, and laundry room cabinets are important focal points of a home. They need to be in great shape. If, after cleaning, they still lack pizzazz but are in good shape, you can refinish rather than replace. Refinishing entails stripping off the old finish, sanding, and staining or painting a gloss white. You can also reface with a new wood veneer or laminate or replace only the doors and hardware. If you don't want to refinish yourself, there are companies that come in and do it for you. The options are many. Three websites that can help are: www.homerepair.about.com/od/paintingandpaint/a/refinish_cabnts_2.htm www.alsnetbiz.com/homeimprovement/htseries/paintrem.html www.indobase.com/home/do-it-yourself/refinishing-touches.html
Bathrooms	These can be tricky. Check around the toilet, tub, or shower and sink to make sure water has not leaked under the flooring and caused the subfloor to swell. If there's damage, replace the subfloor before installing new vinyl or tile. Sinks or tubs with damaged spots can sometimes be repaired with a porcelain touch-up glaze available at any home center. Other options are to refinish the entire tub and replace the sink.
Laundry Rooms	Similar to bathrooms, washers sometimes overflow and damage the floor so you'll need to replace it. Make sure the faucets are in good condition and exhaust fans work. One big problem home inspectors often find is unvented dryers. An improperly or nonvented dryer can cause several problems. Dryers should be vented to the outside, if yours isn't, you may want to check with a plumber or appliance service center. For more information on venting, go to: www.alsnetbiz.com/homeimprovement/dryervent.html
Electrical	This is an area inspectors and appraisers focus on because it's a major safety concern. If your electrical system is old and still uses fuses, you may need to consider rewiring the home. Additions, upgrades, and other projects that involve wiring many times contain hidden problems because installers take shortcuts. If you have an older home, you may want to get an electrical inspection and correct any problems upfront.
Plumbing	After the electric, plumbing is a major concern. If you have an older home, you may want to have a plumber inspect your system. Areas to look for are visible signs of occurring or past water damage, code violations, and substandard connections. Also look inside toilet tanks to see if float valve assemblies and other parts are corroded and need replacing. Turn-off valves to the faucets and toilets need to be checked for corrosion and turned on and off a couple of times to make sure they work smoothly. Three interesting how-to plumbing websites are: www.bobvila.com/ArticleLibrary www.homerepair.about.com/od/toiletrepairmaintenance www.fluidmaster.com

Getting Rid of Mold

Wherever there's water or moisture in a home, you're sure to find mold. In more humid areas, it can pose a health hazard as well as create selling problems. Check with your insurance company and see if the policy covers mold. And if you live in a high mold area, have an inspection before putting your home on the market. Many sales have evaporated when buyers were informed by their home inspector of mold problems.

Mold and mildew are interchangeable names for thousands of species of filamentous fungi. Clusters of these spores can be brown, black, blue, green, and even pink or white. Some are fuzzy while others look slimy.

Molds typically grow at temperatures between 32 and 95 degrees Fahrenheit, but some are active in the 70s and 80s. They require either water or a relative humidity above 60 percent and feed on dead organic materials. Paint, wallpaper, and dust in ducts and wood surfaces can harbor mold.

As a byproduct of digestion, molds release volatile aldehydes, alcohols, and keytones that give them their musty smell. If the temperature and humidity drop and mold stops growing, the odor usually stops too. It hasn't gone away, it's just dormant and waiting around for good conditions to come back.

A keen nose and a flashlight are the best tools to find mold. The following are some mold-hunting tips:

- If mold is growing behind a wall, odors flow out through electrical and television outlets. Remove outlet covers and give the area a smell test.
- Look for water that may be coming from plumbing leaks, plugged gutters, or basement/crawl space leaks.
- Check in the attic along the eaves and at joints under flashing. Look for discolored wood and rusty nails.
- If you smell mold in the ductwork, you'll need to hire a professional cleaning company certified by the National Air Duct Cleaners Association. Check out: www.nadca.com or www.healthand energy.com/air_duct_cleaning.htm

To get rid of mold, outfit yourself with rubber gloves, goggles, and a HEPA respirator equipped with a chlorine cartridge. Mix up a solution of one ounce of ammonia-free detergent (remember ammonia mixed with chlorine releases a deadly gas) to a quart of bleach and three quarts of water. Wet the moldy area for a few seconds and rinse well.

Incidentally, before you can move on to the next section on painting, all surface mold has to be cleaned off or paint won't stick.

Painting for Dollars

One of the most visible and important things you can do to make your home more attractive is give the inside a new paint job. Understandably, this can get controversial. Artistic homeowners and serious interior decorator types sometimes feel the advice to go with white or neutral colors is boring, that agents who recommend these colors lack savvy and panache.

In defense, it must be pointed out that the way you live in a home and the way you sell it are different. Painting a home in light neutral colors encourages buyers to envision their decorating touches, their colors, their furniture, and their pictures on the walls.

In other words, your creative paint choices may make your home uniquely you, but a buyer is probably envisioning another area of the color wheel that's uniquely her. The bottom line is why make it harder for a buyer to write a deposit check?

One home-selling couple didn't believe this when they put their home on the market. They loved color so much that they painted each room a different color: bright yellow for the kitchen and the bedrooms sported pink, blue, green, and salmon hues. Each room was a separate universe and they made no attempt at tying everything together to create a flow. It was a jarring psychological experience walking from room to room. Buyers would take a quick look through the house and out the door to the next home on their list.

After a few weeks with no offers, the homeowners reluctantly came to grips with the feedback the agent passed on from buyers who had looked at the home. Time was running out, so the sellers and their agent decided to offer a $2,500 painting concession. Still, no takers. Buyers didn't like the idea of moving in and undoing someone else's mistakes, although several expressed interest in buying the home if it were discounted about 10 percent.

In the end, the sellers had to leave the house vacant and make payments for four months before finally accepting about a 15 percent discounted offer. Their paint job cost them thousands of dollars and months of lost selling time.

Sellers of another home loved pink—well, the wife did but her husband was colorblind so he didn't care. The exterior was grey brick trim with pink-tinted stucco. Downstairs it was mauve carpet, upstairs it was baby blue. Walls throughout the house sported a pink tint and drapes accented it. If you were into pink, it was a beautiful house.

How couples reacted to the décor when they went through became almost a cliché. Women loved it, but their boyfriends or husbands wouldn't come right out and say that pink stinks. Instead, they would find some other problem, real or imagined, to move on to the next home.

Offering several thousand dollars for a painting allowance didn't help either. And because of the home's good location and great condition, the listing agent didn't feel reducing the price was the way to go. It boiled down to a numbers game, eventually someone would go through who adored pink.

Well, after two months on the market someone did go through who liked pink. In the buyer's words, "I love the house and the decorating and I don't have a husband to veto my decision, I'm buying it for me." Her husband died about a year before, and she had just sold their home of nearly twenty years (painted to her husband's taste—all white).

The important point here is that it took two months to sell a home that should have sold in a week or two because the décor appealed to only a small segment of buyers.

Obviously, it's better to broaden the sales net as much as possible. Maybe there's something to be learned from the ice cream industry. Interestingly, vanilla takes the top ice cream sales spot at 29 percent and the next highest is chocolate at 8 percent, according to the Inter-

Painting and decorating your home in light, neutral colors to appeal to the widest buyer pool is a marketing tool. It's not a reflection of your tastes or decorating savvy.

national Ice Cream Association. Could it be that's why plain "vanilla" décor works so well with the biggest number of homebuyers?

If you need to recoat your walls to bring them back to "factory specs" (that's white), giving them a first-class, professional-grade paint job is not that expensive or difficult. Attention to detail and taking care of the prep work are the secrets. Suggested colors are (of course) white with a tint of brown or grey. Flat paints tend to hide small imperfections and are great for bedrooms, living rooms, and family rooms. Semigloss works well in baths and kitchens. Gloss white paint on trim contrasts nicely with slightly tinted flat wall paint. For ceilings, go with a high-gloss ceiling paint. It reflects more light into the room and makes it look larger.

Finally, go with a good quality brand such as Pratt & Lambert, Benjamin Moore, or Sherwin Williams. Quality paint costs around $20 a gallon; it not only looks better but brushes and rolls on much easier.

Some suggestions on how to make your paint job look great are:

- Cover the floor, furniture, stair woodwork, and anything that you don't want painted with drop cloths. Stray paint droplets have a built-in radar that unerringly guides them to any spaces you leave.
- Remove all door and window hardware, label and store in plastic bags.
- Start with good surface prep. Patch all nail holes and other sheet-rock damage with spackle. Allow to dry and start out sanding with 120 grit, then go to 220 grit and feather the patch work so it blends in with the wall. Sand moldings with a soft sanding block or sanding sponge. When you're through sanding, brush or vacuum the dust off and wipe clean with a tack cloth.
- Apply an acrylic primer for sanded wood and patched areas. Spot priming works if you don't have too many sanded areas, otherwise prime the entire wall. Let it dry overnight and sand lightly with 220-grit sandpaper. Vacuum the wall and wipe down carefully with a tack cloth, any dust left will show up in your final paint job.
- Use a caulking gun loaded with paintable caulk to seal the gaps between molding and walls. Smooth the caulk with a wet finger as you go along.

Five Good Painting Websites

www.ehow.com/how_15_paint-room.html

www.thisoldhouse.com

www.dutchboy.com/painting/index.asp

www.tutorials.com/04/0494/0494.asp

www.paintquality.com/diy

- Paint the ceiling first. Use a $2^1/_2$ inch synthetic-bristle brush or a painting pad to paint about a 4-inch strip around the ceiling perimeter. Take care to make straight lines where ceiling and walls meet.

- For the rest of the ceiling, use a good quality roller with a handle extension.

- After the ceilings, paint the trim and woodwork. Allow to dry, and lightly sand with 220 grit. Wipe off dust with a tack cloth and apply a final coat. Use blue masking tape along the top of the baseboard, after the paint has thoroughly dried.

- The walls are the last area painted. Start by painting about a 4-inch strip with a pad or brush along the top of the wall where it meets the ceiling, along the bottom where it meets the baseboard. Also, paint a strip around windows and door moldings. Switch to a roller and paint the rest of the wall. It goes faster if you keep the extension handle on the roller so you don't have to pull around a stool or step ladder.

- Depending on what you're painting over you may have to use two coats. Don't try to skimp here; if you need two, do 'em.

Many people love to decorate with wallpaper and when you're living in the home, it's great. But come selling time, it's usually has to go. Don't panic, there are exceptions: if it's not outdated, flows with the rest the house, is a decorative stripe dividing a wall at wainscot height or along the top of the wall, you may want to keep it. Wallpaper that's outdated, strong patterned, or an offbeat color screams for removal. Here are some suggestions of getting rid of hideous colors or patterns:

- To start, pull on a corner and hope it peels off in big sections. If that doesn't work, apply a water-based stripper (available at home centers) to dissolve the glue. A garden water sprayer or large plastic spray bottle work well. Spray on a heavy dose and let it soak for a few minutes. The trick is to keep the wallpaper wet as you work to remove it. A wallpaper scraper works well, but be careful not to gouge the wall.

- Once the paper is off, scrape the wall with a straight blade scraper or putty knife. Sponge down the wall until all the glue residue is removed. This is important because paint won't adhere to missed glue spots.

- For vinyl or other hard-to-remove wallpaper, strip the top layer and then soak the underlying paper until the glue dissolves.

- If the wallpaper was applied directly over unprimed drywall, it gets more difficult. You can rip it off along with a lot of drywall paper, but you'll have to skim-coat the wall with joint compound. If you're unfamiliar with this, it's best to hire a professional.

- Apply a coat of primer over the newly cleaned or skim-coated wall. And no, don't even think of painting over wallpaper!

This Old House magazine has a great website that covers wallpaper stripping: www.thisoldhouse.com/toh/knowhow/interiors.

Most homeowners prepping their homes to sell come to the point where they wonder if replacing or upgrading an item should be the way to go. The next section helps you decide if spending those bucks will return your investment.

Upgrades: Which Ones Cost, Which Ones Increase Value?

When the homeowners and their agent came to the kitchen during a walk-through prior to putting the home on the market, the discussion quickly turned to upgrades. The kitchen was sixteen years old and dated: green laminate counters, dark wood cabinets, and a ceiling-mounted florescent light fixture. Even the appliances were original, a little worn but still working.

The agent told the sellers they would need to upgrade the kitchen to sell the home for a good price because it was dated and lacked appeal.

Remodeling was something the homeowners had considered, but never got around to, so they agreed to get several bids and see what it would take to make the kitchen more appealing.

A week later, they went over three bids and decided to go with one that quoted $18,000 to replace the lighting, counters, cabinets, lay new vinyl, and paint the kitchen. Adding another $2,500 for new appliances brought the total close to $20,500.

The remodel certainly did transform the kitchen and make the house more appealing. It sold the first week on the market for full price to a professional couple moving in from out of state.

About a month after closing, the listing agent happened to drive by the home and noticed a lot of building activity. Curious, she stopped and asked the contractor what was going on. He invited the agent in to take a look. She was astounded, they were gutting the new kitchen!

The contractor explained that the couple bought the home because of its location and rambler floor plan that allowed them to design their dream kitchen.

This all brings up some interesting questions:

1. Did the remodel increase the sales price?
2. Would the buyers have bought the home if the kitchen wasn't updated?
3. Did the sellers lose close to $20,500?

In this case the remodel did increase the sales price by the remodeling costs. The home was priced in line with what similar homes in the area had sold for recently, homes that had also been upgraded.

Other homes the buyers had to choose from in their price range didn't fit what they wanted. Location and style were the driving forces in their purchase decision, to get what they wanted, that was the price they had to pay and they did. So, the answer to question two is yes.

It's important to note that if the sellers had refused to do the upgrades, the agent would have recommended a lower sales price. She felt that to make the home more competitive the kitchen needed work. Neither she nor the sellers could foretell what a buyer's motivations would be in buying the home.

The agent also knew that if the home went on the market in substandard condition, the buyer pool would be mostly bargain hunters and investors. Attracting good offers would be more difficult.

In answer to question three, did the sellers lose money? No, they didn't. The sales price was adjusted upward to include upgrades because other homes in that area and price range had kitchen improvements.

Area is always an important factor because buyers are willing to pay top dollar to get in a good neighborhood. That's why many older but desirable areas attract buyers who buy homes and then demolish them to build their dream homes.

You can remodel the home, but you can't do much to improve the location. On the flip side, money spent improving a home in lesser locations won't bring a dollar-for-dollar payback. It may be as low as 40 percent, but in many cases, improvements will help sell the home.

Replacing Appliances

Knowing the age of your appliances can help you make better moving and upgrading decisions. For instance, when you put your home on the market do you include the refrigerator, washer, or dryer or take them with you? If you remodel the kitchen, do you replace the appliances or keep them?

To help you make these decisions, data collected from the National Association of Homebuilders (NAHB) and various appliance manufacturers resulted in the following average life expectancy table. Of course, how long an appliance lasts depends on many factors such as use and conditions.

AVERAGE APPLIANCE LIFE EXPECTANCY	
APPLIANCE	LIFE EXPECTANCY IN YEARS
Air Conditioner Compressor	15+
Dishwasher	10

(continues)

Dryer	14
Electric Range	17
Electric Water Heater	14
Forced Air Furnace	15
Garbage Disposal	10
Gas Range	19
Hot Water Boiler	20–30
Microwave	11
Refrigerator	11–13
Sinks and Faucets	13–20
Toilets	50 years plus
Washer	10–12
Water Softener	20
Window Air Conditioner	10

If you've had an appliance longer that the average life span listed above you may want to consider leaving it as part of the purchase price. Moving costs may be more than the appliance is worth. Check with a local mover for estimated cost of moving refrigerators, washers, and dryers.

Replacing aging appliances is usually a good idea when you upgrade kitchens and baths especially if styles or colors have changed.

Improvements That Bring the Most Return

Since 1988, *Remodeling* magazine has published a "Cost vs. Value Report" that compares construction costs for common remodeling projects with the value they add at resale in sixty U.S. housing markets. You can access this report by going to either: www.remodeling .hw.net/content/CvsV/CostvsValue.asp?articleID = 211765&section ID = 173 or *Realtor* magazine's site at: www.realtor.org/rmomag .NSF/pages/feature1dec05?OpenDocument.

The return on investment that improvements bring when you sell can vary from neighborhood to neighborhood and depends on what your neighbors have done. This is one time when keeping up with the Joneses makes sense.

To help you keep up with the neighbors, here are some things you'll want to consider in your planning.

1. Have a Realtor pull what other sold homes in your area have done. Note the difference in the sales price between homes that have improvements and those that don't. This will give you a ballpark idea if adding a family room or attic bedroom will break even.

2. Check out homes currently for sale in your neighborhood. Go through and note what upgrades the owners have done. If, for instance, everyone has upgraded with granite countertops, then you'll likely have to go that route too.

3. Don't automatically assume that if you pay $12,000 for an upgrade and the research suggests that you'll only get your money back, that it's not a good investment. Remember, the whole is often greater than the parts. Adding another bath or bedroom may allow you to position your home at the top of market rather than in the middle. That can add a few thousand dollars more to the sales price and shorten the selling time.

4. The key is to be slightly better the competition; for example, going with two- or three-color paint jobs, coordinating color flow from room to room, matching appliances, and upgrading lighting—in other words, making changes that don't add a lot of money to the project but create more wow factor.

5. Since house values can vary from neighborhood to neighborhood, it would be wise to talk with an appraiser who is experienced in your area to fine-tune your expectations for return on investment. Ask Realtors and mortgage lenders for referrals.

The following chart will help you in planning upgrades:

UPGRADE PLANNING CHART	
ITEM	UPGRADES
Bathroom Remodel $8,000 to $10,000	Replacing the tub, sink/counter/vanity, toilet, tub surround, light fixtures and flooring should return just about all your investment in

(continues)

	most areas. Adding a bathroom can return more of your investment if you have fewer baths than other homes in your area.
Kitchen Upgrade $8,000 to $16,000	If your upgrades compare favorably with what other owners have done in your area, you should get more return on investment. Give extra attention to the lighting; this is not an area to economize.
Kitchen Appliances $2,500 to $3,500	Go with midprice appliances. Keep the quality balanced—don't install a Viking range with the rest of the appliances from a discount appliance center. Return on investment should be 80 to 100 percent depending on area.
Adding Attic Bedroom $30,000 to $40,000	If all the homes in the area have four bedrooms and you have three, adding a bedroom will usually bring your value up close to your investment. However, adding a fifth bedroom may return 10 to 20 percent less than your investment depending on the area market.
Finishing a Basement $30,000 to $50,000	Finishing off a basement can add bedrooms, baths, family room, laundry room, and almost double your living space. Your return depends on the norm for your area. If most of the other homes have finished basements, you'll get a good return in the 80 to 90 percent range. But, if you're the only finished basement in your neighborhood, your return may drop to 50 percent or less.
Adding a Family Room $40,000 to $60,000	This can be tricky. An addition added to the side or back of a home that doesn't blend with the architecture usually returns less of your investment than one that does. Before going this route, talk to an appraiser and an architect. If your home has the only addition in the neighborhood, return on investment can be as low as 50 to 60 percent.
Home Office $5,000 to $12,000	Again, this depends heavily on the area. If home offices are the rage in your neighborhood, you'll likely get a 60 to 70 percent return. If not, it can go as low as 30 percent.
Electrical/Plumbing Upgrades	Although not high-profile improvements, these usually return in the 90 percent range. Upgrading electrical service and replacing problem plumbing are also strong selling features. A shiny new 200-amp breaker panel impresses buyers looking at older homes.
Carpeting	Most carpet is replaced before it wears out, but average life is around eleven years. Return on investment is low at 40 to 65 percent because buyers expect floor coverings to be in good condition as part of the purchase price. Worn carpet, can invite low offers. For replacement info check out: www.carpetbuyershandbook.com

Once you've gotten the interior ready to go, the next step is the home's exterior. This is where many homeowners have problems with appraisers and home inspectors. The next chapter will cover how to avoid these problems along with checklists to help you prevent those nasty surprises that pop up a week before closing.

CHAPTER 5

Upgrading Your Home's Exterior

The Saturday open house was scheduled from 11:00 A.M. to 2:00 P.M. Ads were in the open house section of the morning daily and a flyer box near the curb was stocked. Their agent planned on putting out open house signs about 10:30 A.M. directing people from two access roads into the subdivision. Additional directionals with colorful balloons would route people to the open house tucked at the back of a cul-de-sac.

Ron and Sarah hoped today would bring a serious buyer. Their decision to move happened quickly when Ron got a job offer in Anchorage, Alaska and had to be there in a month. That didn't leave much time to pack up all their stuff and arrange for a mover. Ron also needed to find buyers for three partially restored cars parked in the driveway and side yard.

About 9:00 A.M., Sarah started tiding up the home for the open house. She put cookies in the oven—their agent told them that helped make the house smell better—and finished loading the dishwasher.

A large picture window in the house's living room faced the cul-de-sac and as Sarah walked by she saw a car come into the circle, make a loop, and drive out. A few minutes later two more cars drove in, one stopped at the curb and a woman reached out and took a flyer. The open house ad appeared to be working early.

Over the next two hours, Sarah counted more than a dozen cars drive into the cul-de-sac. A few stopped long enough to get a flyer, but most drove slowly around the circle and back onto the road.

Just before 11:00 A.M., the agent set up open house signs and the sellers left to take in a movie and shopping.

The first hour and a half no one came through, although a couple of cars drove around the circle but didn't slow down. Finally, a couple did stop and looked through the house. They asked the usual questions: Why are the owners selling? Would they discount for a quick closing? How long has it been on the market? But no real interest.

When 2:00 P.M. finally came, the agent was baffled by the open house response. He couldn't figure out the lack of interest. Situated on a cul-de-sac in a good area, 2,700 square feet, four bedrooms, three bathrooms, and a family room, the home should stir up a lot of interest.

Just as the agent was about the leave, his broker drove up to see the home and how his new agent was doing with his first listing. As he toured the house, the broker listened to his agent's discouraged tale of a house that nobody wanted. It became painfully obvious why the open house didn't produce interested buyers and what he needed to do was educate his agent fast on what would have to happen before the home would sell.

Taking a legal pad, the broker sat down at the kitchen table with his agent and worked up a list of steps he and the sellers would need to jump-start the sale.

The most critical items on the list were:

- The landscaping needed some serious attention. Where grass should be growing, weeds flourished. The lawn needed restoration and the flower beds needed to be replanted.

- It was obvious the owner liked to work on cars in the driveway. Spilled oil had seeped into it, creating large black splotches that would need an Exxon-size cleanup.
- The brick and vinyl siding needed a power washing to remove years of grime.
- Three junk cars (the owner insisted they were restorable classics) in the driveway and beside the house needed to go.
- Tools, toys, garden hoses, car parts, and so on needed to be cleaned up and put away.
- The west-facing front door had sun damage and needed sanding, restaining, and a clear protective coat.

Fortunately, the inside didn't need too much work. With decluttering and cleaning, it could be in showing condition within a few days. The sellers, motivated by a time crunch tackled the list and got most of it done in less than a week.

Sign calls started to trickle in and several agents took their buyers through the home. At the end of the fourth week, the sellers signed an acceptable offer and left for a long drive to Alaska in a moving van. They also had plans to fly back for the closing a month later, rent another van, and move the rest of their furniture and stuff.

In this case, the home sold, but the disorganized approach added weeks and thousands of dollars to the seller's costs. Had they prepped the home to sell before listing and done some planning, they would have saved:

1. Two $1,600 mortgage payments.
2. An additional round trip to Alaska and a week's travel expenses, $3,500.
3. The stress of prepping their home and moving compressed to a few days, priceless.

Of course, picking a newbie agent because they were in Kiwanis together didn't help. They should have interviewed two or three experienced agents active in the area with solid track records.

Also critical to a fast sale is making the right upgrades. But this can be hostile territory where mistakes can make a big dent in your bottom line. To help you avoid these money sinkholes, the next sections zero in on what upgrades return your investment.

Exterior Upgrades: Cost vs. Value

Upgrades and repairs done to sell a home are much different than those you would do if you were going to live there for a few years. For instance, if you are staying put for a few years, you may upgrade to more expensive siding or thirty-year rather than twenty-year shingles. But if you are doing these upgrades in order to sell, you will increase your profits by going with quality products, not top-of-the-line products.

This is not to say that you shouldn't improve your home. If you stay in a home for a few years and enjoy the improvements, that's great. You have gotten a good return on your investment.

Suppose the unforeseen happens and you suddenly have to sell, will those newer upgrades make your house worth more? Usually not, and here's why:

- Buyers expect a roof in good condition when they buy a home, but they typically aren't willing to pay more for architectural (thirty-year) shingles. Also, upgraded siding, concrete work, patios, and other exterior items usually don't increase value equal to your investment.

- Many times you're competing with new construction and it's like a new car, you drive it off the lot and depreciation kicks in. You may think that all your improvements will entice a buyer to purchase your home instead of a new one. But many times that intoxicating new house smell can be irresistible.

- You're also competing against other homes in your price range. That makes marking up your price when you have the only one in the area who has upgraded to a slate roof, for example, a hard sell.

- Buyers expect everything about a house to be in good condition for a certain price. However, a new roof or other replacement may not return 100 percent, but it does make you more competitive and can swing a sale your way. In a cooling market, this often makes a big difference.

> Cost does not equal value. Cost is what you pay for something. Value is what the market says that item is worth. Value is established by what other similar upgrades have added to the price of homes recently sold in your area.

One homeowner, in getting his house ready to sell, hired a roofer to reshingle a badly deteriorated roof. In this case, twenty-year asphalt shingles would have done the job, but the owner figured an aluminum interlock shingle roof that cost about $,3,500 more would be a good selling point and he would get his investment back.

Several months later when the homeowner sold his home, the appraiser didn't allow extra for the new roof. As he explained to the seller, buyers expect a good roof as part of the purchase price. Because the seller spent too much for a roof in that neighborhood was his problem. He couldn't pass on the extra cost to the buyers.

Does this mean you shouldn't add improvements to your home? Not at all. Just remember that cost doesn't equal value. Cost is what you pay for an item, value is determined by the market. In the above example, replacing a bad roof was part cost because it's normal home maintenance. It's also part upgrade because it increases the home's curb appeal.

To carry this further, if you pay $45,000 to put in a heated Olympic-sized swimming pool to help your kids become competition swimmers, the cost is what you write the check for. If you decide to move and no other homes in your area have pools, the value the pool adds to your home will be a fraction of your investment. That's be-

> If you're thinking of adding a wing, dormers, or second story and the area will support it, it's a good strategy to hire an architect. It may add 10 to 15 percent to the bill, but it'll be worth it and you'll recoup the investment and more when you sell.

cause the housing market in your area and price range doesn't give much value to pools.

Even if you found a member of your swim team willing to buy your home and pay more for the pool, the appraiser and mortgage lender would likely nix the deal. They wouldn't want to get caught with an overvalued property should the loan default. In order to put a deal together, your buyer would have to come up with the difference between sales price and appraisal in cash.

To give you an idea of what common upgrades add to the value of your home, the following table shows average return on investment nationally. Be aware that in some hot markets like Chicago, San Francisco, Orlando, Seattle, New York, and so on anything you do to upgrade a home appears to generate a payback. As one Seattle homeowner said tongue in cheek, "someone splashes graffiti on the fence and the price goes up $5,000."

EXTERIOR UPGRADES

UPGRADE	AVERAGE RETURN ON INVESTMENT
Siding Replacement $6,000 to $10,000	Nationally the average is about 95 percent. Some hot market areas can go up to 150 percent.
Adding a Deck $4,000 to $10,000	Averages about 90 percent. Some areas value decks more or the house market is so hot that the return can be up to 150 percent.
Window Replacement $7,000 to $12,000	Replacing older single-pane window with double-pane windows tends to give a higher return in colder climates. National averages are about 90 percent.
New Roof $4,500 to $12,000	Depending on the area, the return ranges from 50 percent to over 100 percent, if you're in a hot market area. It also depends if you do a simple reshingle or a complete tearoff and replace.
Family Room Addition $40,000 to $60,000	Nationally, the return is around 80 percent. It also depends on how well the addition ties into the home architecture. A bad tack-on can actually lower the home's value. Consult an appraiser before you add on.
Home Office $5,000 to $14,000	Converting a bedroom to a home office can give you an iffy return. If buyers want a bedroom more than an office, your return can be minimal. Nationally it's about 70 percent, but a good conversion in a hot market can return all of your investment.
Sunroom $20,000 to $30,000	These are nice to have, but usually not all homes in an area have them. As a result, the average return is around 70 percent.
Second-Story Addition $60,000 to $90,000	Many homeowners get into trouble doubling their home's size because they overimprove for the area. The return depends on the area

and the end result. If it'll support the upgrade, the national average is around 95 percent. However, before you go this route, check with an appraiser and architect.

Much has been said in the media about *curb appeal*. Realtors, appraisers, and lenders also toss the term around a lot and what they're saying is the home looks good to someone driving by.

Good curb appeal makes the drive-by want to stop and see what's inside. Indeed, it's the beginning of the sale and rarely can you ignore exterior repairs and still get the most money possible.

The next section gives you a checklist for getting your home's exterior in shape. Landscaping, the other half of curb appeal, is covered in chapter 6.

Getting the Exterior in Selling Shape

A red and white metal "For Sale" sign on the front lawn had some dings and a few growing rust spots. It had been there through snow storms and summer heat, and now the maple trees in the front yard were shedding scarlet leaves. For over nine months, the owner had tried to sell his home without success. It was priced in line with other homes that had sold in the neighborhood, but the seller had gotten no offers.

What had started out as a no-rush sale suddenly turned into a gotta-sell-now time crunch. The seller's mother a few hundred miles away was diagnosed with cancer and he wanted to be near her.

The seller's determination to sell his home without professional help evaporated and he called an agent who had sold several houses in the area and had a good track record. She knew what the home needed to make it saleable, but making it happen soon was going to be a challenge.

The lap siding hadn't been maintained in years. Wood showed through peeling paint and the south-facing front had starting to deteriorate. Screen doors had no screens and the entry door also had peeling paint. Landscaping had grown wild or died off long ago. Not wanting to fix-up the home, the seller offered concessions if buyers would do the work, but no takers. It took a lot of imagination to see what this house could look like fixed up. Understandably, buyers didn't even slow down driving by this home.

Undeterred, the listing agent had a remodeling contractor she knew look at the house and work up an estimate of what it would take to put it in selling condition. Interestingly, a lot of clean up, prep, and paint along with landscaping restoration would give the home a selling chance. Estimated costs totaled less than $25,000 to bring the home up to market value and would take about two weeks.

Unfortunately, the owner wouldn't invest the fix-up costs even when the contractor agreed to take part when the home sold. That left the agent no choice but to market to fix-up buyers and investors. A few phone calls to people she knew who bought these kinds of properties brought an offer. It was about $50,000 under market, but the owner took it. His failure to invest in giving the home a facelift cost him at least $25,000 and many months of house payments.

Or, to put it more bluntly, had he invested $25,000 taking care of deferred maintenance, the home would have sold for $50,000 more and he would have netted close to $25,000 after subtracting the fix-up costs. If you add in eleven months of mortgage payments, that adds another $12,300 to the loss.

Once a home attracts investors and fix-up buyers, you usually end up with a lot less money than if you invest in a facelift and market to owner-occupied buyers.

In another instance, the owners of a similar home that needed work had an entirely different attitude. They had a frame home with a full basement and an attractive hip-gabled roof. The original wood lap siding hadn't been maintained over the years and deterioration was getting serious. Landscaping obviously was not a priority either because there were more weeds than lawn and a huge weeping willow dwarfed the front.

Amazingly, the inside contrasted sharply with the outside. An updated kitchen, new carpets, paint, and a finished basement created an attractive interior. But before their agent would put the home on the market, the sellers would have to do something about the yard and exterior. Because they found a building lot with breathtaking lake and mountain views, they were motivated to go along with their agent's fix-it-up list. The five most important items were:

1. Remove the weeping willow tree. It blocked the home's view from the front and made the home look smaller than it was.
2. Reseed or sod the lawn, restore the flower beds, and plant colorful annuals, trim the foundation shrubs down to thirty-six inches.
3. Hire a contractor to side the home with vinyl siding, new soffit, fascia, and contrasting color shutters.
4. Re-side the detached double garage and replace the leaking roof to match the house colors.
5. Rent a power sprayer to clean the walks, driveway, and exposed foundation.

It took about two months to get the home in selling condition and the results were amazing. Green shutters contrasted with pale yellow siding, a lush green lawn with colorful flower beds and matching double garage. The house went from a neighborhood eyesore to the most attractive home on the street. It had a lot of curb and emotional appeal, exactly what's needed to attract homebuyers looking for their dream home.

The sellers spent about $19,700 to make their home saleable. When the "For Sale" sign went up, the owners had three offers within two hours. The home ended up selling for $10,130 more than other homes in the neighborhood. If the sellers had not done the repairs and upgrades, the home would likely have sold for about $15,000 less than similar homes in better condition. In this case the return was more than the money spent putting the home's exterior in selling condition. In addition, the home sold fast so the sellers could move ahead on plans for their new home.

To help you attract buyers looking for a home to live in, the following checklist zeros in on possible curb appeal killers. For additional detailed data on exterior upgrade return on investment in different cities according to *Remodeling* magazine go to www.remodeling.hw .net/content/CvsV/CostvsValue.asp?articleID. Click on Special Features, then click on "Cost vs. Value Report."

EXTERIOR FIX-UP CHECKLIST

FEATURE	ACTION NEEDED
Entryway	Replace any broken storm door parts. Entry doors are focal points and part of that critical first impression. Sand and recoat or replace if it's dated or in bad condition.

(continues)

Handrails	These are high-visibility items. On metal railings, sand all rust spots with wet/dry sandpaper or steel wool and spray at least two coats with a quality exterior spray paint. Take care to protect the deck or concrete with plastic or newspaper and masking tape from overspray. White or black are safe colors for metal.
Porch/Steps Walkways	Home centers have polymer-based cement resurfacers that are formulated to repair cracked, spalled, and weatherworn concrete to like-new condition. Ardex All-Purpose Concrete Resurfacer is one example. Interesting websites on concrete repair are: www.interstateproducts.com www.onthehouse.com/tips/19940528 www.thisoldhouse.com
Siding	Your home's exterior is one of the biggest contributors to curb appeal. You'll want to spare no effort here. The return on investment in most areas of the country comes close to 100 percent. If you have aluminum, vinyl, brick, block, or wood siding, rent a pressure cleaner to get rid of grime. With painted siding, be careful not to damage the paint job if you don't intend to recoat. The pressure sprayer is also a good way to remove old paint on lap siding before sanding and painting. If you need to recoat, a website to help you decide on colors is: www.architecture.about.com/cs/repairremodel/a/pickcolors.htm
Roof	Along with siding, roof condition is a big concern to buyers. If your roof is more than ten years old, get a professional roof inspection and have it available for buyers to inspect. No way should you try to market the home with a bad roof. If you've had leaks in the past but fixed them, document the repairs.
Soffit/Fascia	These need to be in good condition. Replace if needed.
Rain Gutters	Gutters should be in good condition with no leaks, damaged, or missing sections. Paint aluminum gutters if needed. Gutter repair or replacement is really a job for professionals with the right equipment and ladders. Check the yellow pages for pros in your area.
Windows	Upgrading an older home with single-pane windows to double-pane windows gives a high return in most areas. For decorative window upgrades, check out how similar sold homes have fared in your area.
Decks	If it has been a couple of years since the deck was stained, you'll probably need to recoat it. Weathered wood may need to be sanded before you restain. Go with a name-brand coating available at home centers. Also check railings, seating, steps, and decking for boards that need to be replaced.
Patios	Look for cracks in concrete and patch. If you do a lot of patching, consider painting or staining the patio. Home centers have concrete coatings or check yellow pages for professionals who have a wide variety of surface solutions that are cheaper than ripping up and replacing the patio.
Garage Doors	This is a high-visibility item. If the door can't be refinished, consider replacing it. Also, make sure the door opens smoothly and the auto openers work. Buyers frequently open and close the garage door looking for problems.

Detached Garage	Like the house, the garage roof and siding should be in good condition. Sometimes oversized garages don't appraise for what they cost you. If you're the only one in the area with a six-car garage, you may not get a good return. But you'll have a great selling feature that'll attract mechanics and RVers like mosquitoes to a bare leg.
Porch	If you have an older home with a built-in porch, it's important that the woodwork and deck be in good condition. Paint the deck with a porch floor paint and follow the directions on the can. Other wood work should be sanded, primed, and painted with latex or acrylic topcoat.
Exterior Lighting	Buyers notice exterior lighting fixtures. If yours are tarnished, damaged, or out of date, you'll need to fix or replace them. Replacements should match your house style—that is, colonial-style fixtures don't match too well with ranch or modern home styles.

Septic Tanks and Wells

Many homes have septic systems, wells, or both and it's important to buyers that these components are in good condition. A good number of home buyers who haven't owned a home with a well or septic system don't understand what's involved in their maintenance. This is something you don't want to gloss over and not disclose because it can come back to haunt you. A few hundred dollars for an inspection is a lot cheaper than thousands in attorney fees.

If you have a septic system, consider these presale suggestions:

- Have maintenance records available that show: (1) How long it has been since the septic tank was pumped; (2) Who the contractor was; and (3) The details on repairs, pump replacement, and drainage field problems.
- If the tank has not been pumped out in the last three years, call a licensed professional (listed in the phone book under "septic tank cleaners") to check and pump out if needed. Even if the system appears to be working well, sludge may have built up to where waste water is released without sufficient time for treatment and settling. This can result in groundwater pollution or eventual drain field clogging and failure.
- Check for odors in the house, above the tank and drain field. If the system is operating properly, it should be odor free. If the

smell test fails, it can be an early warning sign that the system is failing.

- Make sure the contractor inspects each component: tank, outlets, baffles, and drain field. It's a good idea to be present for the inspection and get paperwork detailing the work done.

If you have a private well, you'll want to get inspections for it also. Since the home's water supply is part of what you're selling, you'll need to document that the well is in good working order. Have the following paperwork available for a buyer to look at.

- Water should be tested every year for coliform bacteria, nitrates, total dissolved solids, and pH levels. If you suspect other contaminants, test for those too. Always use a state-certified laboratory that conducts drinking water tests.
- Copies of well permits, recent water tests, pump and pressure tank warranties, and instruction paperwork. Document the well's capacity in gallons per minute, if possible.
- If you've got a pump house, make sure it's in show condition with all the plumbing, wiring, and electrical connections up to code.

Avoiding Scams and Problem Contractors

Many times sellers find they need to hire someone to take care of problems they can't or don't have the equipment to do. Since it's all too easy to get taken by scammers and crooks—especially with the exterior projects covered in this chapter—the following will help you spot the bad guys who want a sizeable piece of your equity.

In one example, a truck loaded with what appeared to be barrels of asphalt coating and a three-man crew stopped in front of a home with a large asphalt driveway. The driver approached the homeowner out working on the yard and told him they were finishing up a job a couple of streets over, had some material left over from it, and would give him a great deal to recoat the driveway if he paid cash.

By chance, the homeowner was considering patching and resealing the driveway and had bids for around $2,500. But when the man offered to do the job for $1,200, how could he lose?

The owner drove down to the bank, withdrew the cash, and gave it to the foreman feeling smug about how much money he saved. And not wanting to be in the way, he left as the crew started to brush on a dark liquid one of them said was a tack coat.

A couple of hours later the homeowner returned and looked at the driveway. It looked dark and shiny like a newly rolled asphalt road surface. By the end of the day it still looked the same. By the next morning, little had changed; it still looked fresh.

As the owner stood wondering what the problem was, a neighbor wandered over and rubbed his finger in the coating and smelled it. It was used motor oil he told the owner. Being a mechanic, it was something he worked with everyday. The scammers had simply brushed on a coat of old oil and left. Now the owner had a nice mess to clean up, a bruised ego made worse by ribbing from the neighbors, and a $1,200 hole in his checking account.

So you don't have to endure ribbing from the neighbors and a bank account hemorrhage, these tips should keep you from being scammed:

- Refuse to do business with a contractor who won't give you a copy of his license and insurance certificate showing up-to-date liability and worker's compensation.
- Never hire a contractor without a fixed business address, phone book listing, or proof of how long they've been in business.
- Be wary of a contractor who tries to cut corners on the paperwork and talk you out of a detailed contract.
- Be wary of a contractor who tries to get you to pay upfront or offers you an enticing discount if you'll pay cash in advance.
- If you agree to pay for materials upfront, don't write a check to the contractor but to the supplier. And call the supplier first to see if the company or contractor is a regular customer in good standing. Better yet, have the materials delivered to you and pay by credit card.
- Don't fall for that classic scam that you'll get a big discount if they can use your home as an example of their work. In reality, you end

up paying full price or more for substandard work. Good contractors don't go door-to-door looking for business; they've got more than they can handle.

- Another classic scam is a contractor who has a crew in the area or material left over from another job and will give you a super deal. Driveway resurfacing, roofing, siding, and insulation scammers use this one a lot.

- Walk away when a contractor tells you the offer is good only if you sign now.

- Be wary when a contractor tries to get you to upgrade additional items. Sometimes they do find unexpected problems, but if you don't feel right about the proposed solution get other opinions.

- Trust your intuition. If something feels wrong or too good to be true, it usually is.

- Always get three bids from reputable contractors. Check out their work and references.

- Beware when the contractor wants you to get any building permits required.

How to Hire a Good Contractor for Those Exterior Repairs

Hopefully, the foregoing has given you the information needed to avoid home improvement scammers. But suppose you have to replace the roof or siding, how do you find a good contractor and get the best price?

Start building a short list by asking friends and neighbors who recently remodeled or upgraded the same type of work you need done. Another source is suppliers; they know their best customers who have been around for awhile. Be aware that the best tradespeople rarely have to advertise. They get all the business they can handle through referrals and repeat business, so you may have to be persistent and leave more than one voicemail. It doesn't hurt to be a name dropper if you're one of their past clients' referrals.

Narrow your list down to three contractors and have them look at your project. Make sure the contractor clearly understands what work you want done and what quality of materials you want used.

Next, it's critical to get detailed estimates with labor and materials broken down because this is the only way you can effectively compare bids.

Sort through the bids and narrow it down to the one you feel most comfortable with. Also, make sure the contractor isn't juggling too many jobs and you're way down on his list.

Here are some tips to help you sort through the bids:

1. Visit each contractor's current job site. Look for work quality, neatness, how well the site is organized. Even note if the company pickup truck is well cared for or is a beater.

2. Don't always go for the cheapest bid. You may find in comparing bids that the low bidder is using cheaper materials or cutting corners somewhere.

3. If you can supply a list of specific materials, such as brand names, model numbers, paint, and so on, comparing bids will be much easier. For example, a roof replacement could specify twenty-year fiberglass shingles, three-tab at $23 a square foot. Also ask the contractor if he can get the materials you want at a discount.

4. Other items you want to make sure are in the final paperwork are: the contractor's name, address, license number, timetable for starting and finishing the job, payment schedule, and the names of subcontractors.

5. Limit the down payment to 10 percent or less unless a higher deposit is needed to order custom items like cabinets or counter tops.

6. Final payment should never be paid until the job is completed and you're satisfied there are no problems. You should also get lien waivers from all subcontractors and suppliers. This assures you that the contractor has paid these people and they can't come back to you for payment.

Now that your home is decluttered and the outside is in good condition the final project is getting the landscaping in showing condition. This is a critical part of creating curb appeal. This is where first impressions are created and we all know that if buyers don't see the inside, there won't be a full-price offer.

The next chapter shows you how to give your yard a quick makeover that'll create a great first impression.

CHAPTER **6**

Putting Your Landscaping in Selling Condition

Marketers know that packaging can make or break a product. That's why they spend billions on showcasing products and doing everything possible to wow you in the first few seconds. They know if they don't, the product will stay on the shelf.

Fortunately or unfortunately, the importance of first impressions is an immutable law that governs just about everything: getting a second date, a successful job interview, making a presentation, and so on.

In selling your home the voltage of this law is turned up to the max.

For instance, buyers circling around a cul-de-sac or driving past homes make a decision to stop in the time it takes their car to travel about a 150 feet. Even if they slow down and gawk, that's still less than thirty seconds.

Also, most serious drive-bys are going down a long list of homes

There are certain things that govern first impressions that you have no control over such as:

- The area of town you live in.
- What your neighborhood is like.
- Your street and the houses around you, especially those on either side.

This is why the best time to think of selling your home is when you buy it.

to look at. That means they're in elimination mode; they're looking for reasons to cross homes off the list and shorten it to as few as possible. First impressions control their pen.

To carry this further, you might say that curb appeal is all about making it difficult for drive-bys to cross your home off their list. And you start by getting your landscaping in showcase condition, motivating drive-bys to pull over to the curb rather than burn rubber leaving for the next home on their list.

One owner who didn't attach much importance to his yard experienced this when he needed to sell his eight-year-old home. Most of the backyard grew prairie grass and sunflowers, it had never been landscaped. The front yard wasn't much better. It was brown and shaggy with a few untamed shrubs.

Agents in the area joked this home would make a great buffalo ranch and would drive their clients by to show what a good deal other homes in that price range were.

For over five months, the home had a lot of drive-bys but no showings. This was unfortunate because the owner was a carpenter and the inside was amazing. He had installed custom crown molding and wainscoting worthy of an English manor, along with wide-plank, heart pine floors. The kitchen cabinets were custom-made cherry wood with antique brass hardware. Too bad no one could get past the lack of attractive landscaping to see the inside. They would have pulled their checkbook out in a flash.

Eventually, a savvy agent listed the property and had a frank talk

It's important to remember that people buy not only a home, but a dream. It's an emotional trip. Landscaping is part of that mental picture buyers have of their dream home. To get the most money from your home you need to "feed the dream" with green and color.

with the owner and told him what needed to happen if he wanted to sell the home. The agent soon found out why the home had gone through three agents and not sold. She couldn't get the owner to follow through on any landscaping improvement commitments. It soon became clear that he was completely overwhelmed by the "green thumb stuff" as he put it and wouldn't follow through.

In frustration, the agent finally set up a meeting with a landscaper she knew and got the homeowner to put $2,500 toward landscaping improvements. It wasn't a lot for what the yard needed, but it was a start.

The landscaper installed sod in the front yard and added concrete edging for flowerbeds with a few trees and shrubs. He plowed the back yard, power raked it, and sprayed a solution of lawn seed and binder to get the lawn started. It was far from a garden club honorable mention, but it did show that the yard had possibilities.

A few days later, some buyers looked at the home and marveled at the inside but didn't make an offer. They didn't want to take on landscaping either and continued looking for a home with a yard that needed minimum work.

Other buyers looked at the home over the next two weeks and finally a young couple made a low offer. The owner countered offering to split the difference and the buyers accepted.

So what can be learned from this situation? The short answer is that bad first impressions end up costing you serious bucks. Also, if the owner didn't have an aversion to yard work, his home would have sold for about $15,000 more and a lot sooner.

This is not to say that your yard has to be as structured as a Japanese garden or can't have a single crabgrass blade on it, but it does need to be attractive.

Interestingly, many buyers who buy a home partly because of the attractive landscaping don't keep it that way. Some new owners don't realize the effort and expense to maintain an attractive yard; six months after moving in, the yard is on its way back to nature.

True, this is not your problem as a seller, but it's important to be aware that even the most clueless green-thumb buyers respond to an attractive yard. Many veteran agents would agree that if they took the home seller in the above example out home shopping, he would buy a home with great landscaping.

Start with a Plan of Action

The first step in getting your yard in selling shape is to develop a plan of action. This involves two parts. First, walk across the street from your home and try to look at it as a buyer would look at it driving by. What do you see? Shoot some stills with your camera or camcorder and take notes on any problems that stand out.

For example, one homeowner was shocked to see how bad a towering sixty-foot fir made his house look. The previous owners had planted it many years ago as a seedling about eight feet from the house. Now it dwarfed the home and destroyed all sense of scale. Clearly, it would have to go.

As another home seller stood across the street from her home, she was amazed at how out of control her landscaping had become. Foundation bushes grew up past the middle of the windows and lilacs along the fence grew so big they obscured a corner of the house. To get her yard in shape, heavy pruning would be at the top of her schedule that week.

Second, find out how your yard compares with other homes that

If you live in a disclosure state, sales prices are disclosed on the deed. A trip to the county courthouse solves the mystery of what homes sold for if you don't have a friendly Realtor who can pull up data on the MLS database. In nondisclosure states, the sales price is not disclosed on the deed.

recently sold. Drive by similar houses in the area that sold in the last sixty to ninety days. Note the price they sold for and their curb appeal. Next, look at homes currently on the market that are your competition. How does your curb appeal stack up to theirs?

If you find your yard is as good or better than the competition, that's great; you're a leg up on getting your home sold first. Take notes on where your curb appeal excels so you use the info as sales points in your flyers and ads.

However, if you need to do some work on your curb appeal to be competitive, make a list of where you need to improve.

First on your list should be the lawn. Buyers often zero in on this first. If the lawn is green, lush, and recently mowed, it gives them confidence that they'll like the rest of the yard and home.

In fact, several homes that sold for top price had nothing but lush, green lawns for landscaping. No trees, flower beds, or shrubs. The buyers were thrilled; to them the hard work was putting in a lawn and sprinkler system. With that done it was like a blank canvas, they could add the trees and shrubs they wanted.

Here are some tips on making a thick, barefoot-friendly lawn:

- If your lawn is more weeds than grass, it may be easier to start over by spraying with Roundup™ or other herbicide. Yes, you can use black plastic to kill the weeds, but do you have a couple of months?

- Next, rototill the yard and rake the soil smooth into a good seedbed.

- Once you have a good seedbed you have three choices: seed it by hand, hydro seed, or lay down live sod. If you're cutting costs, hydro seeding—a solution of mulch and lawn seed—is a good way

If you're short on time you might want to consider hiring a lawn care company. Check out the yellow pages under lawn care or go to:

www.get-lawncare.com

www.happylawn.com

to go and the resulting lawn often looks as good as or better than sod. Sod is instant lawn, but you pay for the convenience. Seeding by hand is cheap, but not as effective. It's hard to get consistent coverage. Check the yellow pages under landscaping for cost comparisons in your area.

- To jump-start an existing lawn, spreading a nitrogen-rich fertilizer can help. However, you may want to ask a local nursery or extension service for other additives needed in your area. For example, acidic soils may need limestone pellets and western alkaline soils may need sulfur for lawns to green up.

- Every lawn has a few brown spots, but if you have some that are eyesores then you'll need to remove the dead grass and till the area. Rake the soil into a good seedbed and reseed. Cover the newly seeded area with mulch and keep moist until the seeds sprout. You can also cut out the brown area and replace with a section of sod. You'll need to pamper the sod and keep it moist for a couple of weeks until it's established.

- Edging the lawn with a power edger gives it an attractive manicured look. Also consider adding metal, wood, plastic, or concrete edging around the lawn and flower gardens.

- When you mow the lawn, use the grass catcher. Dry clippings scattered over the lawn detract from its appeal. Also, don't cut it too short, set the blade height at about an inch or an inch and a half for thick-looking turf.

- Don't let the lawn dry out. Check with a garden center in your area on how much water is needed weekly.

Landscaping to sell a home focuses on the short term. Its purpose is to showcase the home rather than create permanent improvements like planting shrubs and trees. Lots of green lawn and colorful annuals do a good job. Check out:

www.landscaping.about.com

www.bhg.com

www.gardenersnet.com

After the lawn is on its way adding to your curb appeal, the next items are bushes and large plants. This is probably one of the most neglected parts of yard maintenance. True, it's an ongoing pain to keep shrubs and bushes trimmed consistently, but while the home is on the market this is important.

Start off by looking at your yard again from the curb. Is the view unobstructed or is it difficult to see the home because of jungle? Ideally, the home should be framed by trees and bushes that compliment the house.

Trees planted in front of a house can make it look smaller and block light from reaching the inside. The best way to handle this is with a chain saw and pruning tools. Admittedly, this approach is controversial, but in a competitive market, homes that are trimmed neatly and visible from the curb nearly always sell faster and for more money.

Of course, exceptions to this are homes in dense forests, wooded lanes, and other areas that clear-cutting to the end of the driveway would put you in the firewood business. There are also some areas like Tucson and other water-scarce areas that landscape with sand, rocks, and cactus. If you live in those areas, check out the competition and note how you can be just a little more attractive.

When earth-toned colors dominate the landscaping and home exterior, adding a few splashes of color here and there makes your home a little more buyer-friendly. For example, put bright flowers in colorful containers outside the front door and along the walkway. Add paintings and rugs with lots of contrasting color inside the entryway and look for ways to add splashes of color in the home and around the yard.

We instinctively know that color is important in creating first impressions, and to help keep your green thumb on track and incorporate color in the yard, use the following checklist:

CURB APPEAL CHECKLIST

ITEM	SUGGESTED ACTION
Curb or Driveway Entrance	Make sure the concrete curb and driveway entrance in front of the home are in good condition. If they are deteriorated, check with the city; it may be their responsibility to maintain curbing. Adding a

(continues)

	small planter or two with colorful annuals can send a welcome message.
Driveway	Planting strips along the driveway with colorful annuals in a bed or bark is an attractive way to add color where it counts. Also important: Cracks in concrete driveways should be patched and asphalt drives may need to be resurfaced or sealed. Home centers have patching and asphalt products that do a good job for both types of driveways. Also check out this website: www.hotmix.org/driveways.php
Trees	Normally trees should frame a house not block it's view. If your situation doesn't make this possible, thin the branches to create as much light and as clear a view of the home as possible. Also consider edging around the trees with flowers and bark.
Bushes	These usually need to be pruned way down or removed. Bushes, like trees, shouldn't hide the house but rather compliment its architectural lines. Lilac and rose bushes, for instance, take over too much of the yard and need to be trimmed back.
Shrubs	Many homes have shrubs such as Tams growing along the foundation, porches, and fence lines. These should be trimmed down to about thirty-six inches.
Bare Spots and Eyesores	Mulch or beauty bark is a great cover for flower beds and along fences, foundations, and walkways. If you have a spot where grass won't grow, consider tilling it and turning it into a flower garden. Put some edging around it, plant colorful annuals, and fill in with bark.
Foundations	If your home's foundation looks bare and has mud splattered on it from rain storms, you may want to create a three- to four-foot planting strip. Plant five-gallon-sized shrubs every few feet in a bed of bark or mulch. Power wash the concrete first, though, to get rid of the mud stains.
Fences and Gates	An attractive fence is critical to landscape appeal. If you have a wood fence that doesn't look good, spray or brush on a good quality stain or paint. Broken slats or posts should be replaced. Chain link fences can be improved by spray-painting black or green and adding vertical or diagonal slats woven in the mesh. Fix gates so they work flawlessly and replace any rusted or broken hardware.
Flower Beds	These should be planted with colorful annuals in a bed of bark or mulch. Take lots of pictures of your yard at peak growing season. You'll want these to show fall or winter buyers what the yard looks like in the summer.

One example of the importance of color was when Wes and Carol put their home of twelve years on the market when they retired and decided to move into a townhouse. They both loved gardening and were regulars in the local garden club.

Of course, their yard was breathtaking. In the spring, flower beds along the fence were a kaleidoscope of color with red, yellow, and orange tulips bordered by daffodils and other early perennials. Other flower beds planted with annuals created islands of color in a manicured lawn no one in the neighborhood could match.

The house was nice and well maintained but average in that it had not been updated like some other homes in the area. Since the owners were not in a rush, they decided to put the home on the market and see what reaction they would get. If feedback was negative, they would consider some kitchen upgrades the listing agent thought might be needed to make it competitive.

Well, the home went on the multiple listing service and the third couple that went through that week made a full-price offer and a month later the deal closed. Everyone was delighted and the agent was a little surprised and humbled because he felt they would need to do some upgrades to get a full-price offer.

As it turned out, the buyers were first-time homebuyers who had lived in a drab apartment for a few years and were captivated by the yard's curb appeal. It was their long-time dream yard, and they could do nothing else but make an offer. That the inside was in good condition also helped, but as for the slightly dated décor, it faded into the background as a nonissue.

A few months later the agent happened to drive by the house and the flower beds were a mess. The lawn was no longer manicured and green. The new buyers didn't have a clue about how to take care of a yard.

Yes, it's sad. When you sell a house you are really selling a dream, but the buyer's are the only ones who can live in it. Sometimes the home fits their dream and works out, other times it doesn't.

The biggest lesson learned from this is that people often base home-buying decisions heavily on emotion. As a seller hoping to get the most money possible, you need to tap into that emotion with color and appeal. The alternative is attracting bargain hunters who don't care about color; their emotion is getting a good deal at your expense.

Occasionally, you'll have landscaping problems that are a little harder or more expensive to solve, such as too much water in the wrong place. These are critical because they can kill a sale fast.

Landscape Problems That Can Nix Sales

According to the National Association of Home Inspectors (www .nahi.org) one of the most common landscaping problems is improper grading and drainage around the house. This can lead to water penetrating the foundation and can create problems in the basement or crawl space.

Drainage problems should be corrected before you put the home on the market. If you get an offer and a home inspector flags this kind of problem, you could lose a buyer. Nearly all states have clauses in their purchase agreements that make the sale subject to a home inspection. Not surprisingly, water problems are at the top of the list of what scares buyers into canceling their offer.

Here are some suggestions so this doesn't kill your sale:

- Check your basement or crawl space for water seepage. If it's a serious problem you may want to consult a landscaper or contractor. Installing a sump pump, coating the basement walls with a waterproof coating, or re-grading often solves the problem.

- Before you hire a contractor to do expensive trench work, grading, and drain piping, get three bids. Handle the hiring and paperwork the same way you would a remodeling project. How to find a contractor is detailed in Chapter 5.

- Make sure your rain gutters are working and the discharge water is routed away from the house. Gutter extensions and large flex-plastic hoses that fit the bottom spout can help.

- Look closely at your yard's grade. Is it sloped away from the house at least one inch every eight feet? If it isn't, you'll need to re-grade so it does.

- Check the basement/foundation walls where pipes or ductwork enter. If these entry points are leaking, they can be sealed with waterproof caulking available from home centers.

- Check around basement windows. Leaks often occur when water gets in the window well from sprinklers, improperly placed gutter discharge and grading. If you have a basement leak that you've corrected, be sure to remove the water stains from the walls. Old water leak stains can cause buyers to wonder if you've really solved the problem. Home centers have concrete cleaning products that usually work.

- Check your sprinkler system often. Sprinkler heads get knocked by mowing, people, or pets and can fill up a window well or run down the foundation wall.

Of course if you have drainage or water problems and don't disclose it to a buyer, it can come back to haunt you. When the first heavy rain floods the basement, the buyer's first phone call is likely to be to their attorney.

In one such case, a contractor found a home he and his wife loved and they were going through the home for the second time when their agent suggested they get a home inspection. The contractor told the agent he could do a better job than any inspector and to write up an offer.

The home closed three weeks later and the couple moved in. A few days after the new owners moved in it rained heavily and the basement ended up with a foot of water.

The basement walls had some cracks low down that were hidden by boxes when the buyers went through and they didn't bother to look behind them. Plus, a floor drain was clogged or not working and that allowed water to back up. It was a big mess along with a mad and embarrassed buyer. Guess who he phoned first the next morning? Right, his attorney.

The sellers had filled out a disclosure form but hadn't disclosed the defect in the basement or that the grading didn't drain water away from the foundation as it was supposed to.

In the end the sellers settled, but it cost them to fix the problem plus hefty attorney fees. It would have been far cheaper for the sellers to correct the problems than try to get away with not doing anything about a known problem.

Would a home inspector have caught the problems? In a heartbeat; that's what they're trained to do. Contractors may be good at what they do, but few are trained to look for problems involving all the components of a house.

Other potential problems to be aware of are:

- Trees that are too close to the house and can damage the siding or roof.
- Fences, driveways, or even the house that encroaches on another property.
- Ditches, gullies, unstable earth that could cause problems.
- Runoff problems that regularly occur when there's a heavy storm.
- Damaged sprinkler or irrigation systems when you're selling in the spring.

Sometimes hidden problems pop up at the worst time. In one case, a seller had removed a large tree in the front yard and planted grass on the site. Two years later they sold the home. The buyer hired a home inspector who did a thorough inspection but found no problems.

When the buyers moved in, they turned the taps on full in the upstairs bathtub and two sinks to flush the drains. All the water going into the sewer at once caused it to back up and flood the finished basement.

The new owner called a rooter company who checked the sewer line from the house to street with a mini-camera. In running the camera through the line, they found the blockage about where the removed tree had been. Its roots had infiltrated the sewer line and partially blocked it over the years. Even though the tree was removed the roots remained. The previous owners never had problems because they never ran enough water down the drain at one time to back it up.

A home warranty that was included as part of the sale picked up the cost of the drain work. Luckily, the homeowner's insurance that went into effect the day before paid several thousand dollars for the cleanup. Had the buyers entered the house early, before their insurance kicked in, this could have posed a huge liability for the sellers.

The lesson learned here is if you have an older home or one that is more than ten years old, you need to go the extra mile in inspections. Also:

1. If your have lots of trees close to the sewer line, you may want to get an inspection to check for invasive roots or other problems.
2. Include an extended home warranty as part of the sale.
3. Don't let the new buyer take possession until the paperwork records and the new owner's homeowner insurance is in effect. Check with your insurance agent for details on handling this move-out-move-in period.

The next chapter shows how to pull all the information together and create a selling package. It's show time, the fun part. You're getting close to seeing the results from days of cleaning and decluttering. As one owner said: "Getting four great offers in one day made the effort more than worth it."

CHAPTER 7

Showtime

Pulling It All Together

After you've decluttered and taken care of any inside and outside problems, there are a few more ducks you need to line up before curtain time. The biggest is how to organize your home so it pushes emotional buttons that motivate buyers to pick your home. You want to take the wind out of your competitor's sails and sell your home for more money faster than the one down the street. This chapter shows you how to do that.

As an added bonus, keep in mind that money spent prepping a home to sell usually gets their owners a $5 to $10 return for every dollar spent. That's a lofty promise, but considering that most sellers stick a sign in the turf and call it good makes it a sure bet that you'll easily outclass the competition. In fact, agents call a big percentage of homes on the multiple listing service "dogs" (no insult intended for canine friends), meaning they're in bad condition, cluttered, and don't show well.

Suppose for example, a buyer gets preapproved for a loan, say $360,000. Depending on the market, the agent may pull up homes on the multiple listing service priced from $350,000 to $365,000 for starters. Assume the agent finds thirty-two listings in the area the buyers are interested. About twelve will be quickly eliminated because they are obviously overpriced, on busy streets, or have other problems. Another ten are crossed off the list upon closer scrutiny. They may have bad floor plans, odd-shaped lots, sellers or agents who won't return calls, or uncooperative tenants who refuse to set up appointments to show the home.

That leaves only ten properties the agent can preview first or ask his buyers to drive by and cross off those they find unappealing. The final list typically ends up having three or four homes worth going through on it. If they're lucky, the buyers may find one or two worthy of further consideration.

Sound grim? It is. You can see that if you follow the game plan outlined in this book, your home will stand out like a tarantula on a wedding cake. Actually, if you only declutter your home and do nothing else, you're more than halfway there.

In reality, clutter seems to have a strong gravitational pull that keeps sellers in a low orbit about their stuff. Boxing up unneeded stuff is one of the hardest projects for sellers to do. But if you can break

The Seven Biggest Turnoffs for Buyers When Going Through a Home

1. Clutter and distracting items.
2. Walls need painting.
3. Unattractive colors or wallpaper.
4. Worn-out floor coverings.
5. Dated cabinets, counters fixtures, and appliances.
6. Bad smells.
7. A dirty house.

free of that pull and do it, packaging your home to bring out it's best features is like putting money in the bank. Less is more should be shouted from the rooftops!

Packaging Your Home to Sell

This final step in making your home buyer friendly—assuming you've decluttered and painted if needed—is adding a few props. These can be furniture, pictures, lamps, tables, plants, vases of bright flowers, and so on. Whatever it takes to make the home appealing.

For example, a couple going through homes on their list stopped at one that the owners had carefully prepped. Some of the things the sellers did were:

- Set the kitchen table like they were having a candlelit dinner complete with their best silver settings.
- Clean the kitchen spotless and put out matching tablecloths, hotpads, and towels.
- Put fresh flowers welcoming the buyers in the entryway and on the table.
- Completely declutter, leaving just enough furniture in the rooms to look lived in. The buyers had no trouble discussing where they would put their furniture and if anything would clash with the wall colors.
- Put matching drapes and bedspread in the master bedspread. End tables with matching lamps were turned on.
- Lay a light neutral carpet throughout the home tying everything together; no jarring color change going from room to room.
- Give the home a lot of color, mostly with accessories the sellers would take with them.

Lots of color can be added to the décor by using inexpensive and colorful accessories such as rugs, flowers, matching towels, curtains, and so on. This works better than trying to add color with paint, carpet, tile, or countertops.

Actually, this showing was an ambush. All the husband could say as they went from room to room was, "this isn't a house, this is a home." After spending nearly forty-five minutes, the buyers asked their agent to cancel looking at the remaining two homes on their list and write up an offer. Obviously, the offer was not low.

In another case, the owner didn't want to do anything to make his home salable. He wanted to sell the home "as is" and offer buyer concessions to take care of the problems. He totaled up what it would take to fix up the home and offered it as a concession or cash back at closing.

Interestingly, over the three months the home was on the market, all offers were low and included the concession. It became a no-win situation for the seller. There was no way buyers would make a good offer on the home. They felt a price discount was needed for them to take on an unattractive home and the concessions reimbursed them for upgrades that should have been done.

In the real world, you can't give concessions or cash backs to compensate for a lack of prep work. Serious buyers walk away and roll their eyes at the seller's audacity and bargain hunters gleefully sharpen their pencils.

Sorry to say there are no shortcuts. If you want to sell something for full price it's got to be packaged attractively. Maybe someday sellers will be able to shrink-wrap the home and put a big bow on it too!

Start your prepping by going through the home and taking notes on what you think would appeal to buyers. Ask yourself what you can do to push emotional buttons. Keep it simple and add splashes of color where possible.

Since the "in color" palette differs from region to region, it can be helpful to visit open houses, new home shows, and new subdivi-

Make sure the doorbell or door knocker works and is in new condition. Many a buyer has commented on a nonworking doorbell with something like: "I wonder what else in this house isn't working." Their problem-finding radar switches to high beam immediately.

sions. Notice what colors your area decorators are using and what's featured in local or regional decorator magazines.

Here are some prepping ideas for different rooms in your home and yard to get the creative juices flowing.

Front Yard

This is especially important because it's the first thing buyers see as they drive up. If the yard is in good shape, the reaction will be positive. But there are a few things you can do to kick it up a notch. For example:

- Don't park your car in the driveway or garage. Park it down the street a couple of houses so it's out of the way.
- Replace, repaint, or shine the house numbers on the house or curb.
- Make sure the mailbox is in good condition and attractive. Paint or replace if necessary.
- Flank the front door with potted flowers or small trees.
- Make sure the entryway or porch lights are in good condition.
- Add a new attractive door mat.
- Hang a colorful windsock, flags, wind chime, or other props you think would connect with people in your area. For example, on the coast you could add nautical items like ship's lanterns, buoys, anchors, floats, and netting.

Entryway

A splash of color in the entryway is a good way to start a showing. If you've got room, a potted plant on a small table (or a larger plant on the floor), a painting, a framed mirror, a colorful rug, or a vase will work well.

Neutral painted walls with crisp white molding is a hard to beat combo. If the floor isn't in good condition, tile or wood are good choices. Do-it-yourself (DIY) tile projects are easy and cheap. Home centers rent the tools and some have how-to classes. Even people who haven't done tile before can do a great job and have fun.

Things not recommended are family photos, trophies, more than one or two pictures, other furniture (except for a small table), distracting wallpaper, and drapes (blinds only).

Living Room

Depending on your floor plan, the next room buyers are likely to look at is the living room or great room. The colors of the wall and ceiling paint should continue from the entryway. If you're using certain colors for accessories, carry those throughout the house to help create continuity.

Walking into the living or great room, buyers often focus on the walls first. This is an important moment. If the walls are not in good condition and the corners are chipped and dented, credibility goes out the window. Buyers pause and look around or look at their partner or agent with a questioning look. It's obvious what they're thinking: "What other problems are we going find?" As for a full-price offer, forget it!

The first wall to come into view (primary wall) needs special attention. Some things you can do are:

- Hang a large framed mirror or clock in the middle of the wall.
- Hang one large picture with two smaller ones on either side.
- Paint the wall an eye-catching color. To get ideas, check decorator magazines, decorated new homes, and ask people at the paint store what colors the pros are using.
- If you paint the wall a color, you can use it as a focal point to tie accessory colors together throughout the house.
- Consider putting a healthy green plant about three or four feet high in the corner.

Furniture placement and groupings are also important. When you're thinking about where to put items, think three and five. For example, a sofa, loveseat, and coffee table make a threesome; add two end tables and you have five, then stop. Remember, less is more!

Also, notice how you enter the room and arrange furniture so that the sofa or stuffed chair faces you. They should not be a barrier so that people have to walk around them to enter the room. If it's a small room, try angling the furniture to make the room appear larger.

One common problem is furniture that is too large for a room such as oversized sectional sofas, recliners, and other items. Big screen televisions and entertainment centers that dominate a wall or room are notorious for destroying a room's balance. Most of these items should go into storage, leaving just enough furniture to decorate the room.

To add additional color to the living room, try colorful pillows or throws on a sofa or chair and flowers and accessories grouped (three) on a coffee or end table.

You can also go too far the other way. In one larger home for sale, the entryway led to a huge 19-foot by 23-foot great room with an 18-foot ceiling. The only furniture in the room was a sofa in the middle of the room facing a small table against the wall with a thirteen-inch television. Talk about lack of scale and balance. Buyers who looked at the home would stop and laugh at the incongruity. Their focus was broken and they couldn't get back to seriously imagining themselves living there. It also didn't help that other rooms had odds and ends of furniture and stuff the sellers planned on moving when the home sold.

It's unfortunate this beautiful home in a good neighborhood took way longer to sell than it should have. Chances are, if the owner had rented furniture and given the home some packaging or removed everything and professionally cleaned it, it would have sold much quicker and for full price.

> When Shannon needed to sell her condo, she did most of the things outlined in this section. She also personally tiled the kitchen and bathroom floors along with the kitchen backsplash. She spent less than $500 and the first person who looked at the condo bought it for full price.

Formal Dining Room

Formal dining rooms can have a lot of emotional appeal. There are a significant number of buyers who specifically ask their agent to show them only homes with dining rooms. These buyers may have large families, entertain a lot, or just like a having a dining room.

If you have a formal dining room, you want to make sure it pushes the right buttons of those who have one at the top of their list. For example:

- Many homeowners with dining rooms also have large hutches or buffets to show off their china and silver. If they are too big for the room or make it look smaller, you'll want to move it to storage. Yes, that's a lot to ask, but you don't want to distract the buyer with your silver, china, and the Waterford crystal you got on your last trip to Ireland. And you absolutely don't want to make the dining room look smaller than it is.

- Decorate the dining table with place settings and linens like you would when you host a dinner. This gives buyers a chance to envision what a success their social events can be.

- Don't worry about fancy wallpaper or decorator paint schemes, no matter what you do, it's going to be changed. Remember the mantra, less is more!

Kitchen

From the living room or great room, buyers often head for the kitchen. Hopefully, they're impressed with what they've seen so far and are anticipating exciting things to come.

Of course, the kitchen should be so spotless that germs have to carry their own food supply, and no coffee machine or other appliances are in sight. To keep the ball rolling here are a few other things you can do to up your kitchen's wow factor:

- Tile the backsplash—the wall area between the counter and cabinets—with a colorful tile. If you've got a color that you're carrying throughout the house, include it in the tile.

- Install small accent lights under the cabinets every 24 to 32 inches. When turned on, these lights highlight the tile for a dramatic effect. You can also add a strip of two-inch molding along the bottom of the cabinets to hide lights. Stain the molding to match the cabinets.
- If there's a space between the cabinets and ceiling, put a few colorful vases, figurines, decorator plates, plants, or other items.
- Have matching hot pads, towels, place mats, napkins, rugs, and even curtains if possible.
- Check out decorator magazines for ideas such as towels rolled up in small wine bottle racks, colorful flower arrangements, and fruit baskets. There are an infinite variety of inexpensive props you can use.

Baths

The next big item that buyers frequently zero in on is the bathroom. Like the kitchen, bathrooms should be spotless and uncluttered with a few props to encourage buyers to think how fun it would be to live there.

These props don't have to be elaborate or cost much, a few easy suggestions are:

- Make sure the towel racks, faucets, shower curtain rod, and other metal fixtures match.
- Buy a set of colorful towels to use only for showing. Check out decorator magazines and books for creative ideas on where to place them other than on the obvious towel racks. For example, one decorator likes to put rolled up hand towels in a basket with scented soaps and lotions. On the tub, she'll have another basket with soaps, bath oil, shampoos, and so on. Of course, the containers are chosen for their color, scent, and appeal.
- The mirror is an important focal point. Replace it, if it's too small or in less-than-perfect condition. A large mirror that costs a lot to replace can sometimes be resilvered. Check with glass companies that sell mirrors.

- Also important is the lighting. Put a bathroom vanity strip light above the mirror, if you need to upgrade. These lights come in fixtures with three or more bulbs. The number of lights needed depends on the length of your mirror. For instance, a large five-foot-wide mirror may require a fixture with a six to eight light bulbs.

- Add color and charm to the bathroom with an eye-catching shower curtain. If your shower requires one, consider using a tie that holds the curtain open so buyers can see inside the shower.

Before moving on to bedrooms there was one memorable seller, a middle-aged guy who refused to spend the time and effort to showcase his home. He flatly refused to go along with anything covered so far. The home had to be sold and there wasn't a lot of time to do it, so the pressure was on.

The owner appeared to live in just three rooms, the kitchen, master bedroom, and bath. Two other bedrooms and a bath were unused and their doors were always closed.

The rooms lived in were a mess. Clutter was every where, and to compound the problem the house smelled like goats lived there. The listing agent tried to get the owner to work on cleaning it up, but his reply was, "This is my house, and if people don't like the way I live, they can go elsewhere."

Obviously, this home was going to be a challenge to sell. In fact, it was a bigger one than the agent wanted to tackle so he cancelled the listing and walked away.

In the end, the home never did sell and it went into foreclosure a few months later. It's unfortunate that the owner couldn't understand that selling a home is like selling any other item. Packaging and marketing create sales and if you ignore that reality, it's going to cost you big bucks.

In this case, the home was in a good area. For less than $500 the

As one experienced home decorator put it: making a home attractive to buyers is one-third decluttering, one-third cleaning, and one-third prep work.

owner could have decluttered, cleaned, added a little packaging, and made money rather than losing it.

Bedrooms

You could say that bedrooms are the swing vote. By this time, buyers are either seriously considering the home or have concluded it isn't what they're looking for. If it's the former, the home is now on their short list.

Often, sellers who started out wanting big bedrooms compromise when they find a kitchen, family room, view lot, or something else they can't live without. Priorities can change quickly because emotional neurons can dance around like water on a hot skillet.

Still, bedrooms are important and you want them to push as many emotional buttons as possible. If they compromise, fine; make it as easy for them as you can.

Here are some suggestions for making bedrooms more exciting:

- As mentioned in the decluttering chapter, all furniture except the bed, nightstands, and perhaps a rocker or chair should go.
- The focal point of a bedroom, of course, is the bed. Match the bed to the room size—don't put a king size bed in a small room. Nothing can overcome that gaffe.
- Add a colorful comforter or bedspread along with bed skirting and pillows.
- Hang a picture grouping (3) or a large mirror to break up a bare wall. Mirrors work best when they're opposite a window.

Interesting websites for decorating and showcasing ideas:

www.interiordec.about.com

www.hgtv.com

www.getdecorating.com

www.homeandgardenmakeover.com

www.cozylighting.com

www.housekeepingchannel.com

- Plants make an attractive addition to the bedroom's décor. Green or flowering plants both work well.

- Nightstands with lamps are an important part of a bedroom's charm. Use light bulbs that are sixty watts or less. You want an attractive glow, not a bright reading light. In addition to the lamp, plants, books (no paperbacks), or figurines create a nice touch. But, no alarm clock! You want to convey a peaceful scene and alarm clocks are stress inducers.

- Take down any heavy drapes or curtains that make the room look smaller. Leave only sheers or blinds in place. Admittedly, there are some custom window treatments that look great. If yours is one, keep them. The key here is to make the room as light, cheery, and spacious as possible.

- Children's rooms are not quite so critical in terms of color. To make these rooms attractive, cleaning and organizing go a long way. Colorful stuffed animals, toy boxes, chairs, and other items are great accessories.

- A light fixture with a children's theme creates a nice touch. Like other rooms, these bedrooms should be as light and cheery as possible.

Family Room

Sometimes buyers will go from looking at the kitchen to the family room. For many families this is an important room especially if it adjoins the kitchen. Treat this room as you would the living room: light, airy, and uncluttered.

One item that many buyers associate with a family room is the fireplace. A fireplace is an important focal point. If you burn wood, it's important to clean any soot and dirt off the fireplace facing. Home centers carry products that remove soot and make fireplace surfaces easy to clean.

The mantle also needs to look great. Sand and refinish a wood mantle that needs a facelift.

Additional ways to make your family room attractive are:

- Clean the fireplace glass doors or screen along with the metal frames.

- Get a firewood holder, fireplace tools, an old iron Dutch oven, or other props. The hearth is a great decorating opportunity. But remember the rule of three or five. Less is more, right?

- Place a couple of attractive groupings on the mantel, which is also another great decorating site.

- Place a large picture, flower arrangement, or other neutral item above the mantel. Keep it neutral. No trophies, family photos, or other distracting items.

- Group furniture in a similar way to the furniture in the living room, for instance, a sofa, stuffed chair, and coffee table—think three. If you have wood floors, a large braided rug or rugs can separate the room into areas of interest. Family rooms are usually less formal so create a relaxed, family-oriented setting.

- Lighting, too, is less formal. Lamps, ceiling fans with lights, and indirect lighting all work well.

- One problem sellers often overlook is having an entertainment center too big for the room. A large screen television with surround sound is great, but if it dwarfs the room, it's got to go. You may also have to remove other large furniture pieces like hutches, curio cabinets, desks, and so on.

- For ideas on making family rooms interesting, check out model homes, decorator magazines, home shows, and open houses. Especially, go by open houses in your area; you'll want to reconnoiter what the competition is doing to their family rooms.

In one case, the seller, a great hunter, had trophies of game animals he had bagged from all over the world. It was a fascinating room with mounted heads and rifles on all the walls. Unfortunately, it either

> You never want a buyer to pause and wonder if something is or can be a problem. Clutter tends to make buyers think defensively and wonder what all that stuff is hiding.

turned off buyers from considering the home or so distracted them that they forgot why they were there.

The home languished on the market for several weeks. Although it had plenty of showings, no one made an offer. Finally, the listing agent was able to persuade the seller to remove the trophies and give the room a much-needed makeover. Not long after that, the home sold.

Another buyer turned his family room into a rock band studio. Drum sets, large four-foot-high speakers, electronic gear, and instruments took up every square foot.

Predictably, this home didn't sell either, not until everything was removed and the room was redone. Apparently, buyers were unable to visualize themselves as rock stars.

From the family room, buyers usually check out a finished attic or basement. If you've uncluttered and painted, these rooms are unlikely to be deal killers. Still, you may want to add a few decorator touches or splashes of color where possible.

This also applies to the laundry room. It should be as light and cheery as possible with no clutter.

Typically, after buyers have gone through the home, their next stop is the backyard. It's possible they've made a buying decision by now, subject to any unanticipated surprises and you don't want to give them any now.

Patio/Backyard/Deck

Colorful flowers in pots look great on a patio and deck. It's hard to get too many. If you have an outdoor table in good condition, use it as a prop along with the barbeque. However, few things make buyers more excited than a well-tended yard with great grass. In areas where that isn't possible, the focus will be deck, patio, or pool.

In one home that sold, the kitchen and living room were dated and needed an upgrade bad. Orange laminate countertops, a vinyl floor with a pattern that was discontinued over a decade ago, and dark cabinets made the kitchen a liability.

In spite of these drawbacks, the house was clean, in great condition, had a new roof, and was decluttered. The yard was terrific with an oversized pool. A concrete patio wrapped the pool and a manicured lawn with colorful annuals in well-tended gardens made the yard look like it belonged on a magazine cover.

In addition, the pool had an automatic, child-proof cover, diving boards, and all kinds of water toys. Lots of flower pots, attractive furniture, and outdoor lighting added further to the patio's charm.

The first few buyers who looked at the home were captivated by the backyard and had no trouble imagining themselves having fun in the pool. But, alas, reality has a way of getting in the way. When these buyers went back into the house, it hit them like a dip in ice water: the house would need a major update to match the pool—no way could you invite your friends over for a pool party.

After two months of fruitless showings, a couple looked at the home and made an offer. It was a lot lower than the asking price because they essentially discounted the price by what it would take to upgrade the kitchen. It was because of the yard that they were even willing to make an offer.

The sellers had run out of time and reality had started to intrude, as it eventually always does. Their agent pointed out that they should have updated the kitchen long ago, but obviously resources went to the pool and yard instead, which, unfortunately was heavily discounted because there were few pools in the area.

Lessons Learned

1. Keep your improvements balanced. In the above example, so much money went into an improvement that was heavily discounted, it cut painfully into the seller's equity when they sold.

2. That the home was in top condition, decluttered, and clean made a big difference. Not so much in price, but in giving the buyers confidence to make an offer. They didn't want to buy a home that could have hidden problems and turn into a money-eating alligator.

3. True, the buyers enjoyed their pool for a few years, but the loss divided by the four years they had the pool equals about $15,000 a year.

4. When you add an improvement to a home, do some homework first and make sure the neighborhood will support the investment upon resale.

5. Keeping the home in good condition and prepping it for sale did prevent a bad situation from becoming worse. Showcasing a home to show its best is never a mistake.

Additional Backyard Suggestions

- Declutter the backyard and mow the lawn.

- Set the picnic table as if you were having friends over for a barbeque.

- Arrange furniture on the patio or deck attractively.

- Hang colorful windsocks, windmills, and other outdoor items to give the patio color and motion.

- If you have a pool, make sure it's cleaned and the water is clear. Fix any cracks in the Gunite, vinyl, fiberglass, tile, or other liner material. It's usually a good idea to keep the cover in place while showing to minimize the chances of someone falling in. If the buyers are interested you can remove the cover.

With your home showcased and ready to go, the next chapter shows you how to get the word out that you have a great home for sale. It also walks you through the nuts and bolts of how to show your home. This is heady stuff, letting other people see what you've created with your hard work and knowing that they'll be impressed.

Marketing Your Home for a Quick Offer

Now that you've detailed your home and it's ready to market, there's going to be a certain amount of apprehension. You'll ask yourself questions like: Will they like my home? What if they don't like what we've done to it? Will they make a good offer? This is normal preshow jitters and it goes away after a showing or two.

This chapter shows how to minimize those jitters and get the word out that you have a great home for sale. The first part covers the pros and cons of letting an agent do the market or handling it yourself. Either way you'll need to find buyers and persuade them to come and look at your home.

The second part is what to do after they come by. You might say it's about buyer relations and how to show your home at its best. Hopefully, this is a short experience measured in hours, or at most, days. The goal is to get a good offer by the fifth preapproved buyer who comes through.

Advantages of Using an Agent

Cynthia, a single homeowner who had detailed her home beautifully, told her agent that she wanted to be completely insulated from the sales process. She didn't want to be there when buyers came through. The thought of buyers coming through and bad mouthing her decorating and home was something she didn't want to deal with.

If you feel this way, going with an agent is your best strategy. Dealing with lookers, people who find fault with your home, and those who want to lowball your price can be emotionally stressful.

Even with an agent representing you, if your home is prepped to sell you'll minimize selling stress because you'll attract more serious buyers. Bargain hunters will look at your home and know they can't lowball your price and go bother sellers whose homes are messy and smell bad.

There's a lot of hype floating around about why you should or shouldn't work with an agent. Cynthia's reason is she didn't want to be bothered dealing with buyers up close and personal. Others feel they can get more money at closing if they sell their home themselves.

There's no easy answer because of the dozens of variables in play. However, according to the 2005 National Association of Realtors *Profile of Home Buyers and Sellers,* a survey of 7,800 random sellers revealed that those who used an agent averaged 16 percent more money than sellers who didn't.

This confirms what most experienced agents already know: A skilled agent not emotionally involved and with good negotiating skills usually gets sellers more money.

Other reasons you may want to use an agent:

- From a security standpoint, using an agent is often safer because they usually screen their buyers and accompany them showing your home. You lose all control of who goes through your home when selling it yourself.
- Some buyers seek out unrepresented sellers hoping to get a better deal. They know sellers sometimes don't have good negotiating skills and they try to take advantage of that.

- Agents usually have their buyers preapproved for a mortgage before they show them your home, which cuts back on financial roadblocks later in the process.

- Agents do all the marketing and paperwork, and insulate you from dealing with buyer headaches.

- An agent can free you from having to stay home and handle calls and showings.

- One of the biggest pluses is an agent can cast the wide net of the multiple listing service and it's thousands of agents in your local association to find a buyer.

Should you decide to use an agent, it's important to find one that's professional, experienced, and has a track record in your area. Using a friend or relative who just got their license can be a hassle, cost you money, and lead to hard feelings.

The narrowing down and decision-making process for finding an agent should be the same as finding a surgeon, attorney, gardener, house cleaner, or money manager. No way should you use an agent just because she is your friend's niece, sister-in-law, or whatever. Having a real estate license means you've passed a test; it doesn't automatically convey experience or ability to get you the most money.

In one case, a homeowner whose company transferred him several states away listed with a friend who had recently gotten his real estate license. The inexperienced agent priced the home according to what the sellers felt their home was worth. A home down the street sold for $345,000 and their home was much nicer so it must be worth at least $395,000, and that's what they listed it for.

The agent never looked at what similar homes had sold for the last few weeks or checked the competition. The owners arrived at their

Few agents have the experience to work with you in showcasing your home. It's usually to your advantage to do the homework and put your home in selling condition before you hire an agent to do the marketing. That's what they're trained for, that's what they're good at.

price by what they needed to get in order to buy into another home and add in the new roof and the upstairs carpeting they recently replaced. Nothing was even said about prepping the home to sell.

During the office tour of new listings, several agents commented that they felt the home was overpriced but didn't push it. They probably didn't want to hurt the newbie's feelings or dampen his enthusiasm.

In the end, the owners had to move and leave the house vacant. Four months later after making double payments—the house payment and a rental in their new city—they came back and got a professional appraisal that came in at $325,000, which in reality left them with little equity. It was an ugly situation; they lost thousands of dollars in mortgage payments and a friendship. Make sure your agent is experienced. See Chapter 1 for complete coverage on how to pick an agent and price your home.

Selling on Your Own

There are some situations when selling your home yourself can save selling fees and increase your closing check, namely:

- When you know the buyer and there's no problem with them qualifying for a loan. For example, selling to a friend or family member where the price and terms are set between the parties. Sometimes the seller carries the financing and banks are not involved.

- When the market is so hot that, as you plant a "For Sale" sign, a line forms.

- The market is warm enough that you don't need help finding a buyer and you have real estate-related skills from working in mortgage lending, title work, appraising, and so on.

- You're not in a time crunch. If you have a month or two, you can try selling on your own and go with an agent if it doesn't work out. This can be effective if you showcase your home and price it realistically at market value.

- If you don't have any equity built up, you may not have too much choice unless you're willing to pay selling fees out of your pocket.
- A close relative is a real estate broker and willing to help you sell for free.

Attracting Buyers: Getting the Word Out

You may have a great home: spotless, decluttered, priced right, and you're excited and ready to go. Now all you have to do is get the word out and snag a buyer who can qualify to buy your home.

Marketing your home isn't as difficult as joysticking a Mars rover through a crater, despite what many people believe. At least it isn't if you use effective tools. And interestingly, the five most effective tools are not only the easiest but the cheapest. They are signs, flyer boxes, flyers, ads, and referrals.

If you go the "For Sale by Owner" (FSBO) route, this section will show you how to use these tools. Should you decide to list with a Realtor—now or later on—this marketing know-how can help you keep your agent on the ball.

Signs

These are one of the most effective market tools you can use. If you polled all the experienced agents you would likely find more of their listings sold from sign calls than any other tool.

So how can you make signs work for you effectively? Some suggestions are:

1. You want a sign that catches attention and has a readable phone number to people driving by. The minimum-size sign should be 18 inches by 24 inches. Your phone number should be no less than four inches high.
2. Spend a few dollars to get professional lettering. A marker scrawled phone number on a generic red/white sign doesn't give a good impression. You're asking buyers to make an investment worth hundreds of thousands of dollars. Does a sloppy sign encourage that?

3. The main purpose of the sign is to get interested buyers to call you for an appointment to see your home. Some FSBO signs have so much information that it's hard to find the phone number. Don't clutter up the sign with bedrooms, baths, amenities, price, and so on. Too much info can prejudice buyers into eliminating your home from consideration.

4. Put your cell number on the sign. This makes you accessible for appointment calls when you're not home. Calls can come anytime and you don't want to miss a buyer because you were out shopping. Buyers often cruise neighborhoods they like and park in front of homes they find interesting and call for info on their cell phones. At this point interest is high and if they get a recording or no answer, you could lose a good prospect.

5. If your city or town allows directional signs on corners and main roads, by all means plant a few. In this case, generic "Home for Sale" signs with an arrow work great. You don't need any info written on them. Their sole purpose is to guide buyers to your home. These can be very effective because many buyers prowl neighborhoods of interest looking for signs.

Flyer Boxes

Signs and flyer boxes are complementary tools: the sign brings them in so they'll grab a flyer out of the box. Some tips on flyer boxes are:

- Place the box so it's easy for people driving by to stop and get a flyer. If you can position it so a driver doesn't have to get out of the car, that's even better.

- Put no more than twenty-five flyers in the box so you can keep track of how much traffic you're getting. If lots of flyers are going out but no calls to see the home, there are problems you need to uncover.

- If you're on a corner lot, use two signs and two flyer boxes. You want to make it easy for people to spot your signs and get a flyer.

- Call attention to your house and flyers by hanging colorful string flags from a porch pillar or other tie point to the sign box.

Three sites from which you can order flyer boxes online are:

www.smsproducts.com/brochureboxes

www.plasticfab.com/flyerbox.htm

www.flyerboxes.com

Flyers

Many agents and sellers don't realize that the purpose of flyers is not to sell the house, but to pique buyer's interest and get them to call and set up an appointment to see it. If you put too much info they may prejudge the home and never call you.

So what info do you put in the flyers? First, make a list of amenities that homes in your area offer—that is, what motivated you to buy there. Perhaps you bought because the area is close to transportation, has good schools, is in a sought-after neighborhood, or the size of the homes is large. These are the items you want to emphasize in your flyer.

Next, list your home's strong points, especially those pluses you created in getting your home ready to sell—that it's clean, well maintained, freshly painted, has an updated kitchen, and so on. Serious buyers are keenly interested in knowing what you've done to the house.

Of course, the best flyers aren't much good if they don't get into the hands of prospective buyers. Here are a few ideas on targeting buyers:

- A recent National Association of Realtors study reveals that 43 percent of buyers chose a neighborhood because it was close to family and friends. That means there's a gold mine of potential contacts in your area. To tap this resource effectively, pass out flyers to at least 200 homeowners on your street and on adjoining streets.

- Tack flyers up on neighborhood bulletin boards at stores, churches, and so on.

- Take a supply to work and pass around to coworkers.
- On weekends, plant a brochure box next to your directional signs. You'll need to check the boxes often because flyers go fast.
- Always have flyers with you to pass out as opportunities arise.

Figure 3 is a sample flyer of what info you would want to include.

There's a lot of information that's not included in the flyer and that's because its purpose is to get buyers interested enough to come and take a look. As mentioned before, you don't want buyers to pre-judge the home before they see it. Any veteran agent can relate how often buyers who were reluctant to see a home ended up making an offer after they went through.

Important points to convey in the flyer are:

- You want the buyer to get the impression that this home is well taken care of. If your home and the area is fifteen years or older, this becomes critical.
- Notice in the flyer the emphasis is on the upgrades and remodeling. This will be foremost in the minds of buyers looking in this neighborhood.
- If your neighborhood has a reputation for great schools, you'll want to include that. Buyers often drive streets within desirable school boundaries looking for homes. Many times the school is more important than the house—it's that area thing again.
- Bedrooms and baths are important to most buyers and where they're located: upstairs, main floor, or basement.
- Of course, always put in the price and address. If your street is hard to find include a map from www.maps.google.com or www.mapquest.com printed on the back.

One seller, a professional photographer and graphic designer with access to top-of-the-line equipment, created a breathtaking flyer in full-color and a professional layout worthy of any home magazine cover.

Unfortunately, the home didn't live up to the flyer. It was over-

Figure 3. Sample flyer for getting buyers interested in a home for sale.

Alpine Acres' Cleanest Home
1362 Lupine Circle
$279,750

Exterior
- Built in 1986
- Fiber-cement siding and asphalt roof replaced—2004
- Aluminum soffit and fascia added—2004

Interior
- 2,400 square feet—1,200 up and 1,200 down in finished basement.
- 5 bedrooms—3 up and 2 down.
- 3 full baths—2 up (bath off master bedroom) and 1 down.
- Rock fireplace with gas insert.
- Carpet, tile, and hardwood floors.

Upgrades
- Fiber-cement lapsiding replaced 2005—50-year warranty.
- New furnace/central air—2004
- Kitchen remodel: cabinets, counters, range, and dishwasher—2003
- Kitchen floors replaced with tile—1996
- Baths upgraded with tile and new fixtures—2001
- Living room carpet replaced—2006
- Main floor professionally painted—2006

Yard
- .30 acre year (90' x 161')
- 6-foot vinyl fence
- 8' x 28' RV pad with electric hookup

Schools—Alpine School District
- Woodcrest Elementary
- Hillside Middle
- Viewmont High

For Appointment Call Jim or Sandy at 555-3445

priced and needed work, something that wasn't apparent from the photos. In an attempt to compensate, the seller offered several thousand dollars in concessions for problems she didn't want to take care of. Her attitude was: "My flyer will generate enough traffic that I'll get an offer I can work with."

This became an interesting case study for several agents in the area. Would a dazzling flyer make up for other problems? It didn't. The home stayed on the market for several months and the sellers ended up renting it. Buyers, dazzled by the flyer, would look at the home and feel they had somehow been conned. Credibility was destroyed; buyers walked through, walked out, and never looked back.

The lesson learned here is never try to con buyers when talking to them or working up a flyer or ad. It's better to understate than to inflate.

Ads

Ads can be an important part of your marketing mix. Buyers drawn in by ads see your signs and grab a flyer. If they like your flyer's data or your home's curb appeal, your cell phone will ring. It's all designed to do one thing and that's to get buyers through your front door.

When Alberto and Amee decided to sell their home, they had their agent work up a list of competing homes in their area and price range. They toured all seventeen homes on the list and took notes and digital photos.

Amazingly, the sellers found that only five homes were serious competition. The other twelve homes were dumps; they had clutter, needed upgrades that hadn't been done, or their yards were a mess.

Analyzing the five homes that were in good shape, Alberto and Amee found areas where their home excelled, areas that were roughly equal, and a couple of areas where the other homes were better. Alberto and Amee's home had a big yard—the biggest in the subdivision—an extra bedroom downstairs, and their kitchen showed better.

With this gathered intelligence, the sellers and their agent worked up ads and flyers emphasizing that they had the biggest yard in the subdivision, more bedrooms, and a remodeled kitchen. Not surprisingly, this home sold before the others did on the list.

Remove Your Shoes, Please

1333 Aspen Hills Dr. Centerville

Immaculate 2,800 sq.ft. ranch, 4 bdrms, 3 bths, 3-car garage.

Remodeled kitchen and baths.

$489,900   555-1277

When you're putting together an ad, ask yourself what is the number one, most desirable, most exciting thing about your home? What you come up with is your ad heading.

For example, if you live in a highly desirable area because of a certain school, you might write a heading: *Crestview Elementary Area* or *Walk to Columbia Elementary.*

Or suppose you've looked at most of the homes for sale in your price range and area and they're dumps, you can then emphasize how clean your home is.

By looking at the competition, you can adjust your ads to exploit their shortcomings and highlight your strengths. If you've decluttered and showcased your yard, you've got curb appeal that'll ensure appointment calls. Other strengths you can highlight in your ads are address, square footage, number of bedrooms or baths, location within a subdivision, RV parking, two-car garage, and so on.

Once you've written your ads, the next step is to determine what papers will give you the best return for the buck.

Dailies are usually expensive and your ad can easily get lost in a sea of similar four or five liners. However, they do give you wide exposure and that's what you're paying for.

Another option, local weeklies, give your ad longer shelf life, less competition, and usually more bang for the buck. Many people who live out of the area and want to come back get copies of these local weeklies and scan the ads.

Super Clean Cape Cod

Professionally painted and cleaned. 4 bdrms, 3 bths, dbl garage.

Woodland Hills area.

$269,900   555-1277

Your ads can also be effective on Internet sites. Every area has hundreds of sites on which you can upload your ad, sponsored by universities, businesses, television and radio stations, community groups, and so on.

Referrals

Word-of-mouth can lead to a fast sale when you tell neighbors, co-workers, friends, and everyone you know that your home is for sale. Keep plenty of flyers on hand and give two or three to everyone you know. Ask them to pass the flyers on to anyone who may want to live in your area.

In one instance, a seller went around to everyone in her cul-de-sac and gave them flyers. She told the neighbors this was their opportunity to pick their new neighbor and wanted them to know before the sign went up.

One of the neighbors had noticed the sellers prepping their home for sale through the decluttering, fixing up, painting, and cleaning stages with interest. When one of the neighbor's coworkers mentioned they were house hunting, it's easy to guess what happened.

These home buyers were presold by the seller's neighbor before they even previewed the home. As it turned out, they loved the home and made a full-price offer. So was this an isolated case? Not really. As mentioned earlier 43 percent of homebuyers choose a neighborhood to be close to friends or family. That puts the odds of a quick sale much higher than the lottery.

Another seller passed out flyers to her condo neighbors. Later that day she got a call from some friends of a nearby unit who dropped by with an offer and deposit check. They had been waiting for a unit in that building to come on the market.

Word of mouth is so effective that it's a good idea to let neighbors

It's not luck or coincidence that homes prepped and showcased sell quickly and for full price. Neighbors and friends spread the word that here's a home you gotta see. Buyers' skepticism is on a lower setting and they respond to a clean, decluttered house.

and friends know what you're doing to get your home ready to market. Talk about the fix-up, cleaning, painting, and so on. The more they see what you're doing, the more their tongues wag.

If you're having a garage sale, put together a presale flyer to hand out to those who stop by. The flyer can list some basics like square footage, bedrooms, baths, and a few amenities. Nothing elaborate, just enough to get the word out that your home will go on the market in a couple of weeks.

Still another family waited until their home was ready to market before having a garage sale to get rid their excess stuff. They had listed the home that morning and their agent planted her "For Sale" sign just before the garage sale.

Two hours into the sale, a man drove up and asked to see the house. As he walked through he became excited and wanted to make an offer on the spot. The sellers called their agent while the buyer paced impatiently waiting for her to get there.

Interestingly, this buyer had looked at three homes in the area before seeing the garage sale sign and drove by out of curiosity. The homes he had just looked at were cluttered, needed paint, and one smelled of an unemptied litter box. To make it worse this buyer hated cats.

In that light, it's easy to understand why he got so excited and didn't want to lose the home.

Between the time you decide to sell your home and the time the sign is ready to go up will likely be a hectic few weeks. The next step—sort of a payoff for all your hard work—is showing buyers through your home. This next section shows how to do that and to avoid the pitfalls many sellers run into.

The Art of Showing Your Home

Whether you sell the house yourself or list it with a Realtor, showing your home is a critical step in the process of getting an offer.

If you've decluttered and prepped your home as covered so far, showing can even be fun as you discover what buyers think of all your hard work. But don't go suicidal if a buyer comes through and badmouths your home. Some buyers use that as a negotiating gambit; they think this tactic softens up the seller hoping to get the price down a bit.

One buyer lost a home he wanted by bad-mouthing a home in front of the sellers. He hoped to get a slight price break by pointing out every flaw he could find, some real, others imaginary.

When the buyer's agent came back with an offer, the sellers checked the rejected offer box and signed it. Normally when an offer is close, sellers will counter, and give the buyers time to respond. In this case it went back to square one and before this obnoxious buyer and his agent could respond, another offer came in and the sellers accepted it.

Security Concerns

If you've listed with a Realtor, he will likely screen and have his buyers preapproved for a mortgage before showing them homes. Plus, he will accompany them through the homes. This is safest way to sell your home if security is a concern.

On the other hand, if you decide to sell your home yourself, you need to take the following security precautions so you don't become a victim:

- Show your home by appointment only. You'll probably get people calling you from their cell phone parked in front of your home. Do you want to invite them in? Absolutely not if you're home alone! Set up an appointment when other people will be around.

- If you have a showing appointment and no one else is around, get a neighbor or friend to come over.

- Create a log and get names and phone numbers of everyone who comes through.

> If you list your home with a Realtor, emphasize that you don't want to show your home to buyers who have not been preapproved for a mortgage loan. Your goal is to sell your home, not waste time with lookers and tire kickers.

- Jot down license plate numbers of people who not only look at your home but those who park out in front and call you over their cell phone.

- Remove all valuables and prescription and nonprescription drugs and put them in a box in some out-of-the-way place during the showing. If you've decluttered, there shouldn't be much of value to tempt someone casing the house.

- Never show the home after dark. Serious buyers are unlikely to make an offer on a home they can't inspect.

A favorite tactic bad guys use at showings and open houses is for two or more people to come through at the same time. While one or two distract the seller or agent, the other cleans out drugs or anything that's easy pickings. You can counter this by having more than one person in your house when people are walking through.

The Fine Art of Handling Appointment Calls

Calls from your marketing can come at any time, so you'll want to keep your cell phone handy and fully charged. Some callers only want to know the price and a few other details; others will be more interested and want to look at the home.

However, you'll definitely want to screen calls. If you don't, you'll end up wasting a lot of time showing people through who have no intention of buying your home or simply can't buy it. You want to narrow it down as much as possible to those who are serious and can buy.

So how do you do that? Just like Realtors do so they don't waste time on tire kickers: You ask questions. Not so you sound like an interrogator on an episode of *Law and Order*, but in a friendly, chatty way.

In fielding a buyer call, three things you want to know before you make an appointment are:

1. What price range are they looking for?
2. Are they renting or do they currently own a home in the area?
3. Have they talked to a lender and been preapproved for a mortgage yet?

Calls typically go something like this:

Caller: *I just drove by your sign on Elm Street, how much you asking?*
You: *$296,700. Is that the price range you're looking for?*
Caller: *Pretty close.*
You: *Good, do you live in the area now?*
Caller: *Yeah, we're renting down on Ocean View. We moved from Denver a few months ago, and figure it's time we looked for a house.*
You: *That's great, have you talked to a mortgage lender yet about how much you qualify for?*
Caller: *We applied at Arbor Capital Mortgage last week and they said we could go up to $300,000.*
You: *Super. We are available to show the home around 10:00 tomorrow morning or would later in the afternoon work better? Yes, 4:30 in the afternoon would work great, by the way what number can I reach you at in case we have a problem? And your name is? Good, thank you, Phil. See you tomorrow at 4:30.*

Suppose the caller had responded to your question about talking to a mortgage lender with:

Caller: *No. we're just starting to look.*
You: *Well good, I can appreciate that, but we've had so many calls that we're trying to limit showings to buyers who have been preapproved for a loan. Would you like the name of a good mortgage lender that we've worked with?*

Likely the result of this question will be a dial tone or the caller mumbling something and making a quick exit. This approach may

> Selling your home is actually like setting up a business involving hundreds of thousands of dollars of your money. The more professional you treat it, the smoother and more profitable the result.

sound controversial, seem a little heavy on chutzpah, and might steer potential buyers away.

Perhaps, but then you don't have time to follow up on questionable buyers for the next week and see if they really qualify. Your focus is on finding a qualified buyer ready, willing, and able to buy your home—now! If someone wants to whine that you're cherry picking, let 'em.

Sellers who get bogged down with problem transactions or have deals fall apart weeks after thinking they sold their home have usually tried to work with buyers who were not preapproved. You don't want a hopeful buyer's problems becoming your problems.

One couple who listed their home with a Realtor told of previously working with a buyer trying to get a loan. The flaky buyer and mortgage company strung the sellers along for three months trying to put a loan together.

When the agent asked the sellers why they went along with this for so long, they said the lender kept telling them just one more week and he would have it approved. Even worse, these sellers said they didn't want to walk away from a full-price offer their unqualified buyer had given them.

As for working with buyers who are moving up and have a home to sell first, it depends on your timetable and the local market. A seller moving up with a home to sell may have a lot of equity and good credit. If it's a hot market, their home can sell quickly, and you can close both sales the same day. There's more on how to protect yourself in these situations coming up in the next chapter.

With calls coming in from buyers and appointments lined up, the next step is showing your home. How to do that is next.

Tips for Showing Your Home

If you've done everything recommended so far in prepping your home, showing it becomes much easier. It's just a matter of a quick pick up, vacuum the carpets, and wipe off the counters. When the home is decluttered, freshly painted, and packaged attractively, what's not to like? The following tips will make showing the home go smoothly.

- Have a data folder available for buyers to scan while they're there. Have a copy of a professional inspection report. If there are problems that have been corrected, document them. Include summaries of the past year's utilities bills, photos of the home during spring or summer if you're selling in the winter. Also include roofing inspections, septic tank servicing receipts, and any other paperwork that will make your home appealing to buyers.

- Keep a supply of twelve-ounce bottles of water in the fridge and give one to each person who comes through. One enterprising homeowner even made up wraparound labels with color pictures of her home and phone number and attached them to the bottles.

- Point out a few highlights then let the buyers walk through the home on their own. You don't need to accompany them from room to room with nonstop chatter. Give them space so they can relax and focus on imagining how it would be like to live in the home. Tell them you'll be in the kitchen or family room if they have any questions.

- Remember, don't show the home when you're there alone. Have a neighbor or family member around.

- Go easy on the scent generators, such as candles, plug-ins, stick-ons, and sprays. A clean home needs few of these items. Buyers aren't dumb, heavy scents distract and make them wonder what you're covering up.

Don't get too chummy with people coming through and talk too much. Many sellers cost themselves thousands of dollars by shooting their mouth off and saying things that give buyers ammo to make low offers.

For example, six questions that you want to give vague answers on are:

1. When do you have to be out? Tell them it's not definite yet.

2. What's your loan balance? Tell them you're not sure, you'll have to get a payoff from the bank, and then change the subject. You don't want them figuring out how much equity you have.

3. Would you take less? Tell them to make a written offer and you'll look at it.

4. Why are you selling? Simply state that you're moving out of state, to another city, or to a bigger home.

5. Would you pay some of our closing costs? Reply that if they make a good, written offer you'll look at it. Never discourage offers by saying no. Your stock answer should be, "Put it in writing and we'll take a look at it." Unworkable offers many times end up successful after a counter or two.

6. Will you leave the fridge, washer/dryer or whatever? Always answer: "Put it in an offer and we'll consider it."

Realize that some people will say negative things or bad mouth your home. Don't take it personally. This is sometimes a bad tactic uninformed buyers use to negotiate or they can just be boorish. Counter their remarks by smiling and ignoring them; it's not worth getting upset about.

Showing Your Home When Working with an Agent

When you get a call from your agent that she wants to bring some buyers through, it's just a matter of straightening things up and getting lost for awhile. This is the big *do*, the big *don'ts* are:

- Don't hang around and follow the agent and buyer from room to room. They'll have a print out with all the information needed to evaluate the home—let the agent do her job.

WWII posters in defense plants reminded everyone to be careful what they said so vital info wouldn't get back to the enemy. In huge letters these posters read:

Loose Lips Sink Ships

Similarly, in real estate loose lips can result in low offers and lost deals.

- If you can't leave, find an out-of-the-way spot and be invisible.
- Don't discuss price or terms with a buyer; refer questions to the showing agent.
- In the event you're asked about schools, neighborhood, neighbors, and so on answer the questions truthfully with just the facts. Don't offer opinions or hearsay. You may heartily dislike the neighbor across the street but keep it to yourself. Who knows, she and the buyer may be future soul mates.
- Don't leave town and forget to let your agent know how to find you. A home can sit on the market for weeks, then the sellers leave for a few days and that's when an offer comes in.

Showing Your Home During the Holidays

Although there are fewer buyers during the holidays there are also fewer homes on the market. Homes still sell and there are advantages to putting it on the market that time of year, such as:

- You'll have fewer showings, but buyers are more serious. They wouldn't be looking at homes if they didn't have to move now. When these buyers look at your home, let them know it's not a problem showing it. Make them feel welcome.
- Holidays are an emotional time and buyers are in a special mood that a decorated home can tap into. Turn on all the lights, light the fireplace, add a whiff of cinnamon or cloves, and let the buyers soak it all in.
- Be prepared for a buyer who wants to close between Christmas and New Year's. Let buyers know this is an option you would consider. That could be a tipping point between your home and another on their short list.

The holiday season is also a great time to have open houses. As Scrooge would probably say, "You might as well get a good return on all those decorations you put up."

Holding Effective Open Houses

Weekends are for freshly mowed grass and open houses. If you've prepped and showcased your home to sell, you'll find open houses are especially effective marketing tools.

When buyers, jaded and fatigued from looking at cluttered houses drive up to your curb, what they'll see will feel like a cool breeze blowing in off the ocean on a 100-degree day. Their zest for home buying returns and they can't wait to see the inside. Let the games begin!

If you're working with an agent, it's just a matter of helping set up a few refreshments and you're out of there for a couple of hours of fun time. But if you're selling the home yourself, it's more involved. You'll have to do it all, but the following tips can make it easier:

- Put as many directional signs on major and feeder streets as needed to funnel people to your house. You can't have too many signs out.
- Fastening colored balloons to the signs help catch attention especially on the major streets.
- Take around flyers to people in the neighborhood a few days before the open house so they have time to tell their friends and relatives who may be interested.
- Hopefully, you've put open house ads in that morning's daily. Write the ad the same way you would other ads by making the most important item your heading. In this example, Wilson is a highly sought after elementary school, so this feature becomes the heading. Actually, you're targeting buyers who have children they want to send to that school.
- Have all the sales forms and paperwork you need to put a sale together, because you'll probably need it.

Wilson Elementary area—1998 Cape Cod. 2,600 sq. ft. 4 bdrms. 3 bths. Great room. $423,000. Open House Sat 11:00–3:00. 336 Sea Breeze Ct off Oceanview Parkway.

- Follow the showing suggestions outlined earlier in the chapter.
- Greet people at the door and allow them to wander around and soak in the amenities your home has to offer. If they're interested, you'll know it quick.
- Have a good supply of flyers to hand out to buyers as they enter the home.

Somewhat controversial is what food or drink should you serve people who come to your open house. Many agents feel that you should serve something that keeps people on the premise as long as possible; coffee, tea, or finger foods that must be consumed on the spot, for example.

More lavish spreads can send a desperate message to savvy home-buyers that the house needs to be sold. In reality, no amount of gourmet food will sell a cluttered, dirty, or overpriced dump.

So what's the suggested open house fare? Keep it simple with twelve-ounce bottles of water and individually wrapped fitness or granola bars. The goal is to sell the house not create for yourself a big cleanup project. If a buyer comes through who likes the home, not serving caviar won't kill a sale.

Suppose you have a buyer who comes through your open house, loves it, and wants to make an offer: What do you do then? That's what the next chapter is about, how to handle and work with offers and counteroffers.

Working with Offers and Counteroffers

This is one of the most exciting chapters. It's the culmination of all the prep work. The end result of surviving eye-watering, nose-numbing, brain-killing, bleach-based cleaners. Hopefully, no more painting, fix up, marketing, and nail-biting for a while.

When buyers make an offer, it's a validation of your decorating, marketing acumen, and persistence. The doubt and the pain go away. It all worked the way it is supposed to—you've reached nirvana!

However, there's something you should be aware of. Buyers sometimes go through your home and rave over its cleanliness, decorating, and how well it shows. They even spend an hour talking about where their furniture will go and how well the floor plan fits their lifestyle. Wow, you think and start looking around for a pen. You're excited because they're going to make an offer.

After taking up an hour or two of your time, these buyers leave with a firm promise to get back to you in a couple of hours after they talk to their banker. You wait around most of the afternoon expecting their call. It never comes.

You've just met some professional shoppers; spam is their counterpart on your e-mail. They're difficult to filter out so you need to develop a detached attitude and not get excited by what buyers say. Agents have developed the skills to weed out these time wasters, but those selling themselves are usually at their mercy. It's part of the game.

Another situation that tests your emotional detachment is when buyers come through your home and act much the same way the spam buyers did. This time, however, they call you back and want to drop off an offer. They do and it's a lowball offer.

You wonder how they could do that, they liked the home so much. You feel anger and it grows the more you think about the work and effort you put into showcasing your home. And these buyers have the nerve to lowball you!

The key to working with buyers is not to take what they say or do personally, it's just the way some people are. Again, it is part of the game, so be prepared for it.

If you're working with an agent, she will insulate you from these buyers and work with you on handling offers that come in through her or another agent on the multiple listing service. However, if you're selling your house by yourself, and a buyer has dropped off an offer, don't panic. This chapter will guide you through the minefield to a problem-free closing.

What to Do When You Get an Offer

Typically, if your home is listed on the multiple listing service, your agent will call and let you know she has an offer from her buyer or one from a cooperating (buyer's) agent. The buyer's agent may present the offer to you and your agent or may fax it to your agent and she will get with you to consider it.

If you're selling yourself, the buyer will likely drop off the offer for you to consider. Either way, you have three options:

1. Accept the offer as written and your home is sold subject to closing.

2. Write a counteroffer on what is acceptable and send it back to the buyers.

3. Sign on the reject line, as it's such a bad offer that you're insulted and don't want to counter, and send it back.

Option one, of course, is the offer you hope to get. But alligators lurk beneath the surface, so you'll want to make sure of the following before you accept:

- Have the buyer furnish a preapproval letter along with their offer and make sure you or your agent calls the loan officer and verifies the information. Mortgage company approval letters don't always tell the truth.

- Get a big enough earnest money deposit to keep the buyers serious. Your agent can tell you what's customary for your area. In most markets, one percent or more of the sales price is not unreasonable.

- Deadlines are some of the most important parts of an offer and often cause the most problems. Go over the deadlines carefully and make sure you can live with them.

Deadlines for buyers and sellers in the paperwork are much the same from state to state. What they do have in common is you want to keep as tight a leash on deadlines as you can because your home is off the market during that time.

For example, suppose an offer comes in with a twenty-five-day deadline for the appraisal. The buyers know they have twenty-five days so they take their sweet time getting it done. Suppose further that the appraisal comes in low and you don't want to sell at that price and the buyer walks away from the deal. You've just lost twenty-five days your home could have been on the market or sold to another buyer. For many sellers, that's about $1,000 or more in accrued interest.

Important deadlines to watch out for are outlined in the following table.

IMPORTANT PURCHASE CONTRACT DEADLINES

DEADLINE	DESCRIPTION
Offer Acceptance	This is the amount of time you have to send your reply back to the sellers.
Loan Application	This should already be completed. But if a number is needed, keep no more than five business days.
Seller Disclosures	Most states now require sellers to fill out a multipage form that details the home's condition and discloses any problems. Five to ten days should be enough time.
Evaluations and Inspections	This is a biggie. Ten days should be enough time for home inspectors, appraisers, and so on to do their job.
Loan Denial	This is one you want to keep an eye on. It means that after that date if the loan is denied, the buyers may forfeit their deposit. Preapproved buyers don't need more than ten days, right?
Settlement or Closing	This is when everyone signs the paperwork so the loan can fund, and your deed to the buyer can record and you get a check. Thirty days or less is standard in most areas.
Possession and Move Out	This can get sticky. Once the loan is funded you're working on the buyer's nickel. But if your home is decluttered, moving out shouldn't take more than forty-eight hours after recording/funding unless you have other arrangements with the buyers such as a short-term rent back.

Suppose you receive an offer you don't like but that has possibilities, what do you do? As mentioned earlier, you can counter or reject it, but let's assume that you decide to counteroffer. How to do that is next.

Counteroffer Moxie

Standard programming—*let's go in low and hope the sellers will counter up to their lowest price*—often appears seared into buyer's neurons. Or a relative or friend lurks in the background telling them never offer full price for anything. Knowing this upfront helps you stay emotionally neutral and not take low offers personally—they're just part of the game. No offense intended.

Few offers—unless there's a bidding war on your home—initially

If your home is prepped to sell as covered in previous chapters, you will attract better-quality buyers, the offers will tend to be higher, and the deals much easier to put together with fewer counteroffers.

give you what you want. In a normal market you can expect a counter or two before everyone ends up happy. Interestingly, if you've fixed up your home and packaged it to sell, offers are higher and counters fewer and shorter. Some of the major items you'll likely write counters or addendums on are:

Price is obviously number one. In hot markets and bidding wars, your choice is simply the highest offer. In more normal markets it becomes a little more complicated responding to offers that come in short.

When you counter a low price, reduce your price in small increments, say $1,000 or less. This sends a message that your price is firm, but you'll give the buyers a small courtesy discount for trying. What this really gives them is a way to pay close attention to your price and save face. They can tell their friends how they got a great deal and didn't pay full price.

Many sellers counter a low offer by offering to split the difference. (A common negotiating gambit that many people default to.) For example, if you're selling for $250,000 and an offer comes in for $230,000, you offer to come down $10,000 if the buyer will come up $10,000. You end up reducing your selling price by $10,000.

But suppose you countered back at $249,000. This sends a message to the buyer that you're not a pushover on your price. If they counter back again at say, $240,000 and then you offer to the split the difference between $240,000 and $249,000, you've reduced your price only $5,500.

Low appraisals in hot markets are something that happened long ago when pterodactyls flew around. But in a normal or slowing market, they can happen.

Suppose a buyer comes through your home and loves everything you've done to it; it's his dream home. You've priced the home at the top of the market, maybe a tad higher. However, the bank appraiser can't find any recent comparables with the same square footage, bedrooms, and baths to support your price and the appraisal comes in $4,500 lower than your agreed-on price.

Because the offer is subject to the home appraising for the offer price, the buyer can either walk away or stay in the deal if you'll lower the price to the appraisal. Should you agree to this, you and the buyer sign an addendum changing the price. Done deal.

Another option is the buyer ponies up the $4,500 difference. That makes both you and the bank happy. Obviously, the buyer wanted your clean, freshly painted, and decluttered home enough to do that. Buyers sometimes go the extra mile for attractively packaged homes.

Deadlines are commonly kicked back and forth. As mentioned earlier, the longer deadlines go, the more perilous it is for you. If the buyers have a good reason for wanting to extend a deadline and you can live with it, fine.

Inspections can create a pressure-cooker situation, especially if a home inspector comes back with a list of items that need fixing or replacing a week before the closing deadline.

The best way to handle this potential deal killer is head it off at the pass. As mentioned before, it's best to get a professional inspection before you put your home on the market. You'll definitely want to know what time bombs lurk if you have an older home. By taking care of potential problems before the home goes on the market, you preempt inspection problems when you're most vulnerable.

In one instance, sellers building a new home waited until it was just about completed before putting their twenty-five year old home on market. Luckily, the home sold quickly and the sellers planned on closing both old and new homes the same day.

However, ten days before closing (which happened to be the last day of the inspection deadline) the buyers dropped off an addendum listing a dozen items their inspector came up with that needed fixing or replacing. Some were reasonable, others were nitpicking. The sellers had five days to respond. They were in a bind, the buyers knew it, and went for all they could get replaced. Since the sellers couldn't afford to have the deal fall apart, they went along with the buyer's demands.

Incidentally, the sellers got chummy with the buyers and talked too much about their new home and the deadlines they were under. The buyers used this info to pad their repair and replace list knowing the sellers could hardly refuse. It's worth repeating: Loose lips cost you money.

Typically, when an inspector finds problems the buyer or buyer's agent lists these problems on an addendum and sends you a copy. Depending on your state laws, you have so many days to respond or the buyer can cancel the deal.

For example, suppose the buyers find a faulty water heater before the inspection deadline and send over an addendum asking that you replace it prior to closing. Your state law says you have seven days to respond or the sellers can walk away. If you don't respond by the deadline and the buyers don't cancel, the deal is still valid and on track to close. Essentially, the buyers gave up their right to cancel when you didn't respond and they didn't take the opportunity to walk away from the deal.

Another alternative is when buyers present a list of items they want fixed or replaced and you'll only go with some of them. In that case, you write up a counter listing what you're willing to do and shoot it back to them. If they sign it, it's a done deal. If not, it can go on like a ping pong game until both sides agree.

Contingencies are to offers what commercials are to your favorite television program. You endure one to get the benefits of the other. By definition, contingencies are clauses written into an offer that make it subject to something happening. The foregoing deadlines, inspections, house appraising for the sales price, and so on, are all contingencies.

Your job as a savvy home seller is to look at these contingencies attached to the offer and make sure you can live with them. In reality, just about anything can be tacked on to an offer as a "subject to," but they don't become part of the deal unless you agree to it.

Some of the more common ones are:

COMMON CONTINGENCIES TO REAL ESTATE OFFERS

CONTINGENCY	DETAILS
Third-Party Approval of Property	Buyers want someone to check out the property and give their stamp of approval. Uncle Joe or the builder, for example.

Third-Party Approval of Sales Contract	Usually an attorney or financial advisor. Sometimes it's parents putting up the cash for first-time buyers.
As-Is Condition	Either buyer or seller can use this one. A buyer offers to buy as-is; a seller requires an as-is sale.
Removal of Appraisal Contingency	Use an addendum after the appraisal is completed.
Seller Repairs	After the seller completes repairs, the buyer inspects and signs a removal addendum.
Subject to Seller Buying Another Home	Sellers put this in to protect them from becoming homeless if their offer on another home falls through or if they need to find another home first. A certain amount of time is included.
Subject to Buyer's Home Selling or Closing	A time period or clause that, if another offer comes along, the buyers have x amount of time to perform.
Time Clause	The time given for a contingency to happen, usually a buyer's home selling.
Home Inspection	The offer is made subject to an acceptable home inspection by a professional or anyone designated by the buyer.
Credit Report, Loan Approval, and So On	Contingencies dealing with the loan process. It's best to have time limits and remove them with addendums.

It's not uncommon for sellers who prep and showcase their homes to get multiple full-price offers. That's because when you come right down to it, there aren't that many clean, well-cared-for, and problem-free homes on the market!

How to Handle Multiple Offers

Too much of a good thing, like several offers on your home at once, can bring on a panic attack. Actually, if you've got your home in top-selling condition and it's a hot market, it's almost certain you'll end up with several offers the first day it's on the market. In really hot markets, the decision can boil down to how much over asking price the offer is—10 to 20 percent or more is not uncommon.

Should you be so lucky, here's how you can handle this situation:

1. Have your Realtor inform all parties that there are x number of offers on the property. If you're selling the home on your own,

then you'll be informing all interested parties that you'll look at all offers on a certain day and time.

2. If you're working with an agent, his or her office is a neutral place to meet with the buyer's agents and go over the offers. When you're selling yourself then have the buyers drop their offers off to you by the deadline.

3. Go over the offers and pick out the best one. If it's a keeper, sign it. If not, counter it with a time limit for the buyer's acceptance.

    Next, take the second best offer and also counter it. Make sure you write in the counteroffer that it's a back up offer #2 and will kick in if offer #1 rejects your counter. It should also have a time limit for acceptance. Offer #3 and any other offers are handled the same way.

4. If the first counteroffer accepts, you've got the home sold on your terms. If the buyer of the first counter says no, then the second counteroffer gets an opportunity to accept or reject and so on down the line. With this approach, all parties are treated fairly and you end up with the best offer possible with the least amount of brain damage.

    For example, Todd and Peggy—selling their home themselves—dealt with multiple offers when they sold their $575,000 four-bedroom, three-bath ranch in a superheated market. They decided to kick off their marketing with an ad in an area weekly that comes out on Friday mornings. Five couples came by Friday afternoon and three on Saturday morning. By noon they had four offers in hand and one more on the way.

    So how did these sellers handle this sticky situation?

    First, Todd told each party that came through they would cut off accepting offers at 3:00 P.M. on Saturday.

    Second, at 3:00 P.M., Todd and Peggy sat down and went over the five offers. The first two offers they eliminated. One was less than the asking price, another was subject to a home selling in another state. The remaining three were good offers and both had financing verifications attached. One was for $585,500 with a sixty-day escrow, and the other was $585,000 and a thirty-day escrow. The third offer of $586,000 had a carpet replacement contingency of $3,500.

Todd and Peggy chose to go with the buyer offering a thirty-day escrow because the interest part of their loan payment was $1,540. Add that to their $335 accrued monthly property tax bill and they would lose $1,875 by going with the sixty-day escrow.

So what's a quick way to determine which offer is the best one? It's easy, just fill out the data on the Offer Comparison Worksheet.

OFFER COMPARISON WORKSHEET			
ITEM	OFFER 1	OFFER 2	OFFER 3
Sales Price			
Settlement Date			
Preapproval Letter			
Earnest Money Deposit			
Inspections Deadline			
Appraisal Deadline			
Loan Denial Deadline			
Subject to House Selling			
Possession Date			
Repairs/Replacements			
Buyer Closing Costs			
Down Payment			
Appliances Included			

In the case of Todd and Peggy's three best offers, their worksheet would look this.

OFFER COMPARISON WORKSHEET			
ITEM	OFFER 1	OFFER 2	OFFER 3
Sales Price	$585,500	$585,000	$586,000
Settlement Date	60 days	30 days	30 days

(continues)

Preapproval Letter	Yes	Yes	Yes
Earnest Money Deposit	$5,000	$4,500	$6,000
Inspections Deadline	10 days	10 days	15 days
Appraisal Deadline	10 days	10 days	15 days
Loan Denial Deadline	15 days	10 days	20 days
Subject to House Selling	No	No	No
Possession Date after Closing	48 hours	24 hours	3 days
Repairs/Replacements	None	None	$3,500 carpet
Buyer Closing Costs	None	None	None
Down Payment	10%	20%	5%
Appliances Included	All attached	All attached	All Attached
Subject to Buyer's Home Inspection	Yes	Yes	Yes
Home Warranty Included	Yes	Yes	Yes
Subject to Appraisal	Yes	Yes	Yes

Obviously, offer number two would be the best one to accept. Notice in offer number three that what the big print gives with the $586,000 sales price, the small print takes away with the $3,500 carpet replacement contingency.

When comparing close offers, notice the buyer's down payment. A down payment of 20 percent or more is often a better loan than 5 percent or less down. There's no way to really know because the mortgage lender can't divulge credit scores. But all else being equal, it's usually safer to go with a bigger down payment because these loans are least likely to have problems.

Unfortunately for sellers, markets do not always remain hot and the need for Offer Comparison Worksheets becomes a sepia-toned memory of the good old days. For normal or slowing markets, you may need additional ammo to increase your competitiveness even when your home is showcased to look its best.

Tips for a Highly Competitive Market

A slow market is created by more homes chasing fewer buyers. This kind of market happens when a major employer leaves, the area is overbuilt, the interest rates are high, the local or national economy is in a slump, or even sometimes from bad weather.

Suppose the market in your area tanks. The number of people buying homes drops by 20 percent—an extreme example. But that leaves 80 percent of potential home buyers still making offers. If your home is packaged attractively to sell, you'll still attract buyers.

Sellers who suffer most are those with homes that are in marginal condition, less desirable areas, or bad floor plans.

Competition and more homes in the inventory mean some may catch on to the secrets of packaging their home as you have done. That means you'll need to be a little more savvy and competitive. And concessions can be a great way to make you more competitive.

However, a word of caution: The best way to use concessions is when you're negotiating an offer—a pot sweetener—and not offer them up front.

Here are some things savvy sellers do to sweeten the pot so buyers will make an offer or take your counter:

- As we've discussed throughout the book, the number one sweetener is the home's condition—fresh paint, like-new floors, great curb appeal, and so on. To enhance this you could offer a coupon worth x professional home-cleaning visits.

- Price your home right at market value. Adding so called wiggle room to the price can make you uncompetitive and lose potential buyers in a cooler market. If you're not willing to accept a small price break, address it when an offer comes in. If your home is sharp and showcased, you will get offers where others won't.

- Offer to pay the buyer's closing costs, between 2.5 and 3 percent of the loan amount.

- Throw in appliances or other items the buyers may want. If your appliances are several years old, it may be a plus to replace them with more energy-efficient models rather than to move them.

   In one particular sale the seller threw in a big screen television and a pool table to make the deal work. Fortunately, the buyers went for it because the seller had finished the basement family room after he hauled in the television and pool table. There was no way to get them out short of disassembly or serious demolition.

- If a buyer doesn't like your carpet color or decor, offer to replace it up to a certain dollar amount. Typically, this can run from $2,500 on up depending on price range and area.

  This is different from an allowance that some sellers use to avoid fixing problems like bad carpet or paint. When you do this, you'll likely end up with a bargain hunter wanting the allowance and making a low offer too.

- Offer an extended closing date of sixty to ninety days. This can be enticing for buyers moving from another area where they have to close on their home first. It can also work if the buyers have a few months left on an apartment lease.

- If a buyer has a month or two left on their lease, you can offer to help buy out the lease so they can buy your home.

- Better than extending the closing date is to close and rent back from the new owners for a month or so. The monthly rent would be the buyer's mortgage payment. This could be a plus by giving you additional time to find another home or to build a home. Plus, you've sold the home, closed, the money is in the bank, and your stress level is way down.

- Offer a home warranty. This is a third-party insurance policy that insures the plumbing, heating, electrical, and appliances for a year. Should something go wrong, it'll be fixed or replaced. Typical cost is $250 to $600.

- On the creative side, you can take an asset the buyers wouldn't mind parting with as down payment credit if it would help them buy your house. For example, a buyer loves your house, but lacks a few thousand dollars to make the deal work. Suppose he has a blue Laguna Seca BMW M5 sports car you can't take our eyes off. You learn he and his wife are having twins, so they need a house more than a sports car . . . You get the idea!

  It's important to listen to the buyers who come through. Let them talk and note what their needs are so you can effectively respond to any offers or counters. Likewise, if you're working with an agent have her talk to the buyer's agent and get as much information as possible. This may not be critical in a seller's market, but in a slow market you may have only one chance to make a sale and you don't want to lose it.

Also, listing with a Realtor can be the best way to go in a slow market. They have access to qualified buyers and cooperating agents can hammer out deals that may otherwise never happen. In the end you may not end up losing that much money. It can boil down to paying money in commissions or paying as much or more slashing your price to attract a bargain hunter.

In addition to finding out what buyers' needs are, you can use timing to help you be more competitive.

How to Put Timing to Work for You

When you get an offer you should treat it like opening a can of Pepsi: You've got about an hour before the fizz is gone. Buyers in a slow market often have more than one home on their short list. If you get an offer with a short fuse, you need to know your selling costs and your bottom line so you can respond quickly.

How do you find out these costs?

- Know your current mortgage balance(s). Because mortgage loans accrue interest from the first of the month, you'll need to add a month's interest to approximate your payoff. For example, if the balance on your mortgage statement is $279,500 and your interest rate is 6.25 percent, a month's interest is $1,455.73 ($279,500 × .0625 = $17,468.75 ÷ 12 months = $1,455.73 for that month). Add that to your statement balance for a rough payoff of $280,955.73.

- Check with your mortgage lender and make sure there are no prepayment penalties if you pay the mortgage off early. Subprime and interest-only loans are notorious for having these penalties.

- Call a title company and find out what the title and closing costs would be for your sales price and area.

- Add in selling commissions and property tax proration.

With this information at your fingertips, you can act swiftly with an acceptance or counter. Never assume just because buyers have made an offer on your home that they've stopped looking.

It may be written on the paperwork that you have forty-eight hours to decide, but remember they can withdraw their offer any time before you've signed it. Too many sellers see they've got *x* amount of time on the offer and relax. And many buyers don't shift out of search mode until their offer is signed and delivered. There are a lot of real estate war stories where buyers have made an offer and then stumbled upon another house they liked better. Their agent has to frantically call the selling agent and tell him the buyers are withdrawing their offer.

Experienced buyers' agents often write "upon presentation" in the line for how long the seller has to respond. They do that so the sellers can't use the offer to push a fence-sitting buyer they may have into making a better offer. In real estate speak, this is called shopping the offer.

In short, even though the offer may give you so many hours to respond, think of opening a can of pop: It doesn't take long until the fizz is gone. It's the same with offers. You want to accept or counter immediately to stop the buyer from losing their enthusiasm or further shopping.

In one case, buyers presented an offer to a seller with *upon presentation* written on the Offer and Time for Acceptance line.

The sellers were upset that they had to respond on the spot or the offer would expire. The offer was several thousand dollars lower than the sale price and the owner wanted to get more—a bird-in-the-hand deal versus getting less than hoped for.

Patiently, the buyer sat quietly as the seller whined and complained that the offer was too low and he would like more time to think it over. The buyer told the seller he was sorry but he had other homes to look at and stood up to leave. Instead of letting the deal go, the seller jumped up and told the buyer he would reluctantly sign the offer.

Unfortunately for the seller, he found out a few days later that his mortgage had a prepayment penalty that would cost him an additional $4,500 at closing.

The lesson to learn is that savvy agents and home buyers are going to put short fuses on their offers and you need to have your ducks lined up so you can work the numbers and respond quickly.

In real life no two home sales are alike. Each selling situation poses its own unique problems that require a creative approach. The next chapter looks at some of the more challenging problems sellers have in getting their homes sold.

CHAPTER 10

Solving Difficult Selling Problems

Not all home sales are straightforward. Sometimes problems arise that throw a wrinkle in the best laid plans. This chapter focuses on selling a home under challenging conditions, such as looming foreclosure, divorce, and bankruptcy.

It's not intended to give legal advice, but to suggest marketing solutions to selling properties when these situations arise. Consult an attorney and/or accountant before you attempt to sell a property with a problem. Most often there are legal or tax problems hidden just beneath the surface you need to factor in.

Selling Homes in *As Is* Condition

One common trap unwary sellers fall into is trying to sell their home in *as is* condition. *As is* can mean anything from a house at the bottom of a lake to one that has a bad paint job.

Sometimes sellers try to take the easy way out and don't want to paint, carpet, or fix the leaky faucets, so they offer an allowance hoping to find a willing buyer. Some problems this creates are:

- Homes in not-so-good condition tend to attract investors and bargain hunters. No matter how low you price the home, bargain hunters will offer less and want the fix-up concession too. You may be better off getting bids on how much it would cost to fix up the home. Compare the bids to what the home would sell for fixed up and see if it's a money-making possibility.

- Mortgage lenders have appraisal and condition standards a home must meet. If its condition won't appraise, the only buyers you can attract are those who can pay cash. You know what kind of offers they will make.

- Many states require the seller to fill out a property disclosure form. If the buyer finds problems you didn't disclose, you could incur some hefty legal fees. Before you try the *as is* route, get legal advice on putting together an addendum that covers you.

In one case, a seller inherited a three-bedroom bungalow that needed a lot of work. In addition to a leaky roof, the interior needed new floor coverings and the kitchen and baths needed upgrading.

The seller first tried selling it at a discount, and when that didn't work, he offered several thousand dollars cash back at closing. The only offers were from investors who offered cash but discounted the price 30 to 40 percent and wanted the discount too. The house wouldn't appraise in its condition, so there wasn't a way to finance it so the seller could get all his cash out.

Eventually the owner talked to a broker who knew the area market and suggested he get bids on what it would cost to fix up the house and make it salable. Comparable homes in the area were selling for $190,000 to $219,000. The seller had been trying to sell for $160,000.

Electing to do the cleanup and painting, the owner got an estimate of $30,000 to put the home in salable condition. Over the next thirty days, the seller and contractors fixed up the home, restored the yard, and did a stunning makeover.

The home went back on the market for $212,000 and sold for full price a week later. Had the seller been able to sell the home *as is,* he would have walked away with $160,000. But fixing up the home and selling it, profited him $22,000 more than trying to dump it, which he was unable to do.

Five keys to making these situations work for you are:

1. Know what similar homes in good condition are selling for in the area.
2. Get a home inspection so you know what the problems are.
3. Get bids from three contractors for work you can't do yourself.
4. Work the numbers so you know what total fix-up and selling costs are and subtract that from the projected sales price.
5. The more work you can do yourself, the bigger the payoff when the home sells.

Another selling problem that can cause a few sleepless nights is when you have to sell and your loan balance is higher than the market value of the home. That puts you in the world of short sales.

Short Sales 101

In real estate speak, if your mortgage balance is higher than what similar homes are selling for in your area, you're negative (or upside down) in your mortgage. But if you have to sell your home, it becomes a short sale. These are typically created by situations where:

- An equity credit line or second mortgage that, when added to the first mortgage, puts loans 100 percent or more over the appraisal, or a first mortgage that's a 100 percent or more of current value.
- Home values in your area dropped faster than you could pay down the mortgage.
- The home's condition has deteriorated enough to reduce its value.
- Payments are past due or the home is in foreclosure.
- You've tried to sell the home, but market value or offers you get are less than your mortgage balance.

So what do you do if you're caught in this sticky situation?

The first step is to get your home in top condition so it'll command the most money possible in your area. The less money the bank has to discount, the easier a short sale is to put together.

One couple who had to sell because of a job transfer considered going the short sale route. They had taken out a second mortgage to get rid of high-interest debt on some credit cards. The lender loaned them 125 percent of appraisal over a year ago. That put them about $30,000 over current values. The area had appreciated about 10 percent and after adjusting for that, they were still about $12,000 in the negative.

When they decided to sell, they talked to two agents active in the area and both told them their loans totaled more than the home was worth and they couldn't help them.

Discouraged, the sellers happened to mention to a neighbor their problem and she suggested they call a friend of hers, Gina, who worked for an interior decorator.

Gina handled a new service her company offered, staging homes for builders and home sellers. She was an accredited staging professional and had helped several owners package their homes that sold quickly for top price.

The sellers called Gina and she came out, looked at their home, and called an agent she knew who was familiar with the area. After talking with the agent and looking over the seller's loan balances, Gina felt if they showcased the home they could get about $9,000 over what the other agents said the home would likely sell for. She told the sellers that if they would invest about $700 in decluttering, cleaning, and painting and pay her fee of $500 she would supervise the final showcasing just before they put the home on the market.

For the next month, the sellers hauled stuff to a rental storage, thoroughly cleaned the house, and finally with Gina's help, packaged

Before you go the short sale route, look at what similar homes have sold for in your area. You may be able to prep and showcase your home so it sells for more money.

the home to push as many emotional buttons as possible. Neighbors who looked at the home were amazed at the difference.

Emboldened by the comments of neighbors and friends who looked at their handiwork, the sellers decided to go for broke and price the home at $235,000. This was their break-even price and $12,000 over what similar homes had sold for in the area.

In the first hour, three couples came through their open house and loved the home, but no offers were made.

Two more couples came through the second hour and left without saying much other than they had a few more homes to look at. About forty-five minutes later one of the couples came back and wanted to make an offer. They were preapproved for $233,000 and were willing to offer that for the home. This meant the sellers would have to come up with around $2,000 to close. This was a lot less than the original $12,000 loss, so they accepted the offer.

Luckily, the mortgage company's appraiser felt good about the home too and appraised it for the sale price.

Other Options

In this case, a bad situation ended like an NBA game in double over-time where the home team won. But suppose the situation is too far gone to sell your way out of—then what do you do?

You go the second route: Call your lender's customer service. It's usually an 800 or other toll-free number on your monthly statement. You will be assigned a representative to work with. Lenders don't want to go the foreclosure route unless they have to.

If you see payment problems coming, it's important for you to contact them as quickly as possible and not wait until it gets too big for a positive solution.

Both the U.S. Department of Veterans Affairs (VA) and the Department of Housing and Urban Development (HUD) have programs that work closely with homeowners heading for default. In some cases, the VA and HUD will buy back the loan from the lender and work with the homeowner on a revised payment plan. You have to qualify for these plans, but it's worth it if you're having problems making payments.

The typical route a short sale takes is when the homeowner gets an offer that's close to market value but less than the mortgage balance. The listing and/or selling agent puts together a sales package that's submitted to the lender (the homeowner does this if selling themselves). This package should contain:

- A copy of the filled-out and signed (both buyer and seller) purchase agreement along with a copy of the earnest money check.
- MLS printouts of similar homes that have sold in the last month or two as well as competitive homes that are now on the market.
- A copy of the preapproval letter from the buyer's lender.
- A financial statement or government-approved closing paperwork called HUDs—prepared by a title company—showing how much money the lender needs to forgive so the deal will work.

This package goes to the contact person assigned to the case by the lender. Your proposal will likely go to a committee who decides on approval, rejection, or counter.

Sometimes you'll get a quick answer on your proposal, other times it can take a few weeks and a few phone calls or e-mails to get results.

Also important: Run the numbers on the HUDs or financial statement by your tax advisor before submitting the short sale package. You may find out the sale carries tax penalties you don't want to incur.

Unfortunately, some homeowners in short sale situations make the mistake of waiting to contact the mortgage lender after they've missed two or three payments. That puts thirty- to sixty-day late dings on their credit and makes recovery more difficult.

It's better to work with your lender before you miss a payment. Don't delay when it becomes apparent you may need to go the short sale route.

The effect of a foreclosure on your credit is that you'll have to wait

Run the numbers by your tax consultant before submitting a short sale package to the lender. The IRS may deem forgiven funds a tax liability and that can cost you some big bucks.

three years before you can get another mortgage. Although there are B lenders who will work with you after a year, the price is steep and the terms have some sharp stingers.

The bottom line is a short sale can save your credit from a devastating hit, but be prepared for some extra paperwork and time putting it together.

Divorce Dilemma: Selling Your Home

Short sales are sometimes an outgrowth of divorce. When married, a couple qualifies for a high loan-to-value (LTV) mortgage using both incomes. However, when they split up, one person ends up living in the house and making the payments. As long as there are no hiccups in the income stream to the one making payments, life goes on.

But suppose the cash flow becomes erratic or disappears? In that case, chances are the home goes on the selling block or becomes a short sale candidate. If you're the ex-spouse who lives in the home and makes the payments, the following suggestions will help make selling easier.

- Make sure both of you are on the same page about getting the home sold. Having one ex-spouse getting cold feet or refusing to sign the needed paperwork can cause some sticky problems.

- Get a title report on the home before you list it or put it on the market. If there are judgments that have attached to the property, you need to know if there's going to be enough equity from the sale to clear them. Back child support that's a lien on the property can create a selling problem.

- Read the divorce decree carefully and make sure both of you are in agreement on how the equity will be split—that is, do the math up front not at the closing table.

- Have the title or escrow company work up trial HUDs a day or two before closing. If one of the ex-spouses has to come up with money for the deal to close, you want to make sure that's covered. Have those funds in escrow with the title or escrow company before closing day if possible.

> Some second mortgage lenders are careless about the home's valuation. They go more on credit score than loan-to-value (LTV). As a consumer, you need to be careful you don't end up with more loan than house value.

In one situation, the ex-spouse who got the home in the divorce decree decided to sell it. At the time of the divorce, there were two mortgages on the home, so one ex-spouse quit-claimed her interest to the other in exchange for his agreement to make the mortgage payments.

About eighteen months later when the owner decided to sell, he listed with an agent who was familiar with divorce sales. First thing the agent did was contact the lenders and get payoff amounts for both mortgages. Unfortunately, the payoffs totaled about $10,000 more than the home was currently worth. The second mortgage was a greater-than-appraisal loan that many homeowners get stuck with.

Working the math, the agent did a rough HUD closing statement that showed the seller would need to come in with $14,650 to close. That left the seller three options:

1. Stay in the home and pay down the balances. Because he planned on getting married soon and moving to another state, that ruled out staying put.
2. Rent out the home until it appreciated and the balances were reduced. In this case, the payments were about $400 more than the home would rent for. Plus, managing the home from 500 miles away or incurring professional management fees was not an enticing option.
3. Come up with $14,650, sell the home, and move without worrying about the home.

The seller opted to come up with the money needed to sell. There were too many problems and costs with keeping the home from long distance.

Some interesting lessons learned are:

- When negotiating a divorce make sure you know the mortgage balances and what the home is worth. In this case, the seller agreed to take the home and assume the mortgages without knowing the market value of the home.

- The seller didn't take good care of the home during the eighteen months he lived in it and wasn't interested in prepping the home to bring up the value as much as possible.

- Don't take out a second mortgage for more than the home is worth. Before getting a second mortgage, know your current market value. Lenders often make loans based more on credit scores than on a home's value. In a hot market, appreciation keeps the wolf at bay, but a cooling market exposes the sharp fangs of negative equity.

Another common result of divorce is the home going into foreclosure. When a normal or short sale doesn't work, foreclosure results. But sometimes you can pull the situation out of the fire.

When the Home Is Headed for Foreclosure

Typically, when an owner misses several payments, the lender will file with the county recorder a notice of default. From that moment the countdown begins and depending on the trustee, the owner has about four months before the property is sold at competitive auction. Any time before the trustee sale the owner can redeem the property by paying the back payments, attorney fees, and other costs.

Foreclosure can put a serious ding on your credit, and if possible, it's better to find an alternative solution. For example, one couple, Mike and Rebecca, faced foreclosure on their four-year-old home when he lost his job. Unable to make $1,617 payments on one income, they fell three months behind and the mortgage holder filed a notice of default. That meant they had about three and a half months before a trustee's sale.

Rebecca contacted a broker and made an appointment to come over.

Going over the paperwork from the mortgage lender, the broker totaled up the funds needed to stop the sale:

COST	AMOUNT
1. 6 payments (3 in arrears, 1 current and 2 projected)	$ 9,702.00
2. Late charges (4% of missed payments)	194.04
3. Lenders accrued attorney fees	1,786.00
Minimum amount needed	$11,682.04

It appeared the only way out was to put the home on the market and hope for a fast sale. The mortgage balance on the home was $234,567 plus the $11,682.04 and another $1,742 in closing costs put the breakeven sales price at $247,991.04.

The broker looked at what comparable homes in the area had sold for the last three months. None had sold for over $249,000. That left no room for brokerage fees so the home couldn't be listed on the multiple listing service. Mike and Rebecca would have to try selling it themselves, although the broker offered to help them with the paperwork if they found a buyer. He also loaned them a couple of tapes that explained how to stage and showcase their home.

The sellers, realizing they had a lot at stake, tackled the steps outlined in the tapes. They decluttered, cleaned, painted, and staged the home inside and out. After spending weekday evenings and a couple of weekends the home looked like a model. It was ready for buyers.

Unfortunately, the first open house was a dud. It rained all that weekend and no one came through despite an ad in the weekend daily and lots of directional signs. Two buyers called about midweek after seeing the ad and wanted to see the home on Saturday.

Encouraged, the sellers decided to try another weekend open house and hope for good weather. This time the results turned out better; four buyers came through and one returned later with an offer for $245,000 and a two-week closing.

The two tapes the broker loaned Mike and Rebecca were: *Dress Your House for Success* by BCW Video at www.bcwvideo.com and *How to Prepare Your Home for Sale* by Barb Schwarz at *www.stagedhomes.com*

Mike and Rebecca countered the offer at $248,500 and the buyers accepted it. The deal closed with a month to spare.

With a sigh of relief, the sellers saved their credit from foreclosure, but it would take a year or two of on-time payments before their credit score got up to the mid-700 range again.

Some of the important lessons to learn are:

- Be careful in using both incomes to qualify for a loan. Consider the possibility of one income temporarily drying up.
- Stay on top of home values in your area. If you don't have much equity, take a proactive approach if making payments becomes a problem. Contact your lender before you slide several payments in arrears.
- Consider a short sale early before the costs pile up.
- As stressed throughout past chapters, fixing up and packaging your home for sale is a highly proactive approach that often produces great results.

Selling a property in foreclosure or putting together a short sale is easier than dealing with stigmatized properties, but as we'll see in the next section it can be done.

Selling Stigmatized Properties

It was an attractive two-story home in a great area, nestled in the foothills with a great view. The couple who looked at the home loved it—it was what they had been searching for.

Their agent scanned the listing printout and stopped suddenly at the days-on-market (DOM) entry. It showed seventy-three days;

> Some states don't require you to disclose that a property has a history of suicide, homicide, or has housed a meth lab. If you have a stigmatized property don't despair; it can be overcome. In fact, there are successful investors who buy these properties, give them a makeover and resell for big profits.

something was wrong. This home should not have stayed on the market that long. The agent shrugged, no biggie. A prior sale could have fallen through or a computer glitch.

In the end, the buyers called their agent three days after moving into the home in anger and despair. The neighbors had told them the former owners—an elderly couple—had gone into the basement, disconnected the gas line to the water heater, and committed suicide.

As a result, the owners wanted to sell and discovered local people wouldn't buy or refer people to the home, and local agents wouldn't show it. An out-of-state buyer working with a nonlocal agent had no way of knowing the home had a problem. It was not disclosed on the MLS printout because that state didn't require it.

Many states have laws specifying that agents or sellers are not required to disclose certain nonphysical problems such as suicide, owners with AIDS, or a haunted house. So before buying a home, it's a good idea to talk to a few neighbors and find out if there are problems you should know about.

In this case, the new owners were stuck with no easy legal recourse. They lived in the home for a couple of years and gave it a complete makeover. Feeling the stigma had faded, the owners put the home back on the market and sold it for a good profit. Although they loved the home and area, they never felt comfortable living there.

Typically, most common stigmatized properties are created by:

- Suicide or homicide occurring on the property.
- Previous owner had AIDS or other disease.
- House was contaminated by an illegal meth or other drug lab. Some states require this be disclosed, others don't.
- Home is found to be on a contaminated site from previous mining, industrial activity, or landfill. Even though the area may have been cleaned up, the stigma can still remain affecting home values.
- The neighborhood is a high crime area.

Many times there's not a lot you can do in the short term with contaminated or high crime properties. Stigmatized properties that are the result of suicide, homicide, diseases, and drug lab problems can be handled. How well, depends on the area.

For example, one home in which the previous owner had committed suicide was sold to a rehabber who completely gutted and remodeled inside. When it went on the market, it sold in a couple of days because the home was in a good area and looked great from the remodel.

Interestingly, the buyer was a homicide detective who found out about the suicide from one of his friends at the department. Not too happy about the situation, he called the agent and asked him to meet them at the property.

Since the property hadn't closed, the agent was sure the buyer wanted to cancel the sale. However, when they met at the property, the buyers walked around the property and talked between themselves for about thirty minutes.

The detective's biggest worry was how his wife would feel about the home and could she live there. After discussing it, they both decided to go ahead with the closing.

Their reasons were:

1. The property had been completely remodeled with new floor coverings, paint, appliances, and fixtures.
2. The home was in a good area, and the buyers couldn't find another home as nice in their price range.
3. They knew that in the future the stigma would fade and they could resell the home for a profit.

Would these buyers have bought if they knew the problems upfront? The buyers in the first example wouldn't have closed had they known. However, those in the second example could have backed out, but went ahead and closed anyway.

Not all buyers react to these kinds of problems the same way. But some ideas that help you make the most of problem properties are:

• Even though your state laws may not require disclosure, always disclose problems on the flyer or listing. This brings the problem out into the open where you can deal with it.

- The better the area, the better your chances of giving the home a makeover and overcoming the problem. A remodeled home in a great area will sell as long as the buyers are satisfied all traces of the problem have been erased. Sometimes a discount goes a long way to overcoming buyer resistance.

- Don't skimp on the remodel. If, for instance, the home had a meth lab, the inside needs to be stripped down to the studs. Document the work with photos and documents from the contractor. Keep a detailed log of everything you did to the home; this gives buyers confidence you've solved the problem and they're getting a good deal.

- Help buyers see it's a trade off. They're buying a property with history, but they're getting a much better home for the money and time is on their side. As memory of the problem fades, so does resistance to them selling it later on if they need to.

- If you end up with a problem property, before you panic and sell to a bargain hunter for a steep discount, talk to brokers familiar with the area. Get an idea of what the home would be worth with a complete makeover. Next, get a couple of bids on how much the work would cost. Look at the numbers. More often than not, you can make money taking positive action.

Two more sticky situations that create selling problems are specific to condos and to a lesser extent townhouses.

Condo Ratios and a Cooling Market

Over the past few years, condo sales have broken records every year like there was no gravity. They have even outpaced single-family homes in some areas. But there are two serious traps that condo sellers can fall into.

The first can catch you off guard when you sell your condo and find out the buyer can't get financing because of the ratio of owners to nonowners in your development.

The major players in the secondary market (Fannie Mae, Freddie Mac, FHA, and VA) who buy condo loans from mortgage companies have some strict rules on financing condos. They will not buy loans where:

1. The development has more than 50 percent of the units as rentals. This means that if investors have found your development attractive and own more than half of the units as rentals, your buyer may not be able to get financing at a competitive rate. That in turn means you may have a hard time selling your unit if there's no easy financing.
2. No one owner can own more than half of the units in a development. Small condo projects and conversions would be hurt more than larger developments. For example, if you bought a condo in a small, ten-unit project and needed to sell before all the units are sold, you may have a problem.

So what should you do if you own a condo and are thinking of selling? First, check with the condo association and find out the ratio of owner versus nonowner units. Second, if you have this problem, check with the developer and ask around for lenders who warehouse their own loans and will finance these kinds of projects.

Be aware that mortgage lenders who specialize in condo developments often warehouse loans until the development meets ratio guidelines. Once they exceed the 50/50 mark they can sell the loans to Fannie Mae or other secondary investor.

The second condo trap is when the market cools and units in your complex start sporting "For Sale" signs in the windows. In a good market, this usually isn't a problem. But the painful reality is that the only thing that separates one condo from others like it is price.

Typically, a few owners who have to sell start discounting prices. That starts a downward price spiral and the value of your unit becomes what the lowest priced one is currently selling for.

So what can you do in this situation? First, keep your unit in top condition. If you have to sell, buyers are going to be comparing your condo to others with similar floor plans and amenities. Sometimes buyers make an offer based on colors, carpet condition, or a view out the window.

Look at the units that are for sale and showcase your unit to look better or throw in sweeteners such as furniture, appliances, or paying some buyer closing costs.

Second, if you owe more than the unit is worth, consider becoming a landlord until the market changes. You may end up with a small negative cash flow if you hire a rental company to manage the unit, but that's better than a big ding or foreclosure on your credit score.

To show how the dos and don'ts of the previous chapters come together, the next chapter shows how a professional stages a home to sell along with additional tips to get the most money possible.

CHAPTER 11

Showcasing

How the Pros Do It

As stressed throughout the book, people buy homes based on emotion. Once they find their dream home, they don't want to lose it. Making a low, contingency-ridden offer is a bigger risk than most people want to take.

Many buyers can relate how frustrated they felt when another offer beat out their best effort, especially when they offered more than asking price. Next time, it's no messing around: they're going to look for ways to make the seller happy and richer.

On the flip side, homes that agents and buyers label dumps attract bargain hunters and investors who are not going to pay full value for anything. You and your house don't want to go there. Let the bargain hunters from the dark side find other properties to prey on.

So far, the book has shown how you to prep your home on your own and avoid those bargain hunters from the dark side. However, if you're short on time or don't want to tackle the prepping nuts and bolts, you can hire a staging professional to work with you.

From developing a plan of action to the final packaging of your home to sell, these professionals work with you to supersize your closing check. This chapter will show you how to find, hire, and work with a professional. Also included in it are impressive before and after photos that illustrate what staging can do for your home.

How to Find and Work with a Professional

Home showcasing, fueled by television reality shows, is rapidly becoming a real estate industry. Agents, interior decorators, home renovators, and anyone with a yen to decorate are hanging out their shingle. That means the professional quality runs the gamut from scammer to excellent. So how do you find the best talent? The same way you find it shopping for an agent or contractor. Some sources are: Agents, title people, the Web, open houses, builders, and booths at home shows. Make sure you:

- Check out their track record of how many homes they've staged in the last three months. Get specifics: names, addresses, and references.
- Look at homes they've recently showcased. This is important. You want to be comfortable with the person's style and taste.
- Work up a short list of three home showcasers who impress you as able to walk the walk as well as to talk the talk. Set up an appointment for them to see your home.
- Go over their program and cost options. Go with the one you feel most comfortable with and think can do the best job.
- Having an Accredited Staging Professional™ (ASP) or similar professional designation shows they're serious about their industry.

Once you find a showcasing professional, treat this just like hiring a contractor: Have a contract that spells out exactly what you're paying for. If it's not in writing, it doesn't exist. If you make changes, those should go on contract addendums, signed by both parties.

> Once you decide to sell, your home becomes a commodity—a
> house. It must compete in a free market with other houses.
> Buyers are going to comparison shop and be influenced by
> packaging as with any other commodity. If you ignore this
> marketing reality, you do so at your own peril.

Most showcasers have a fee schedule of services. Typically, at the bottom will be a consultation fee of several hundred dollars for a walk through and working up a list of things to do. From there, fees range up to several thousand dollars for whole-house packaging. Additional fees can apply if you need rental furniture and/or props.

Some home stagers are heavy on the hype and tout claims of homes selling for inflated prices. Occasionally homes do sell for inflated prices, but there is a downside. In one case, a home was showcased and showed beautifully. The owners did get a fast offer, only to have the appraisal come in $10,000 lower than the sales price.

Appraisers have to follow appraisal guidelines and no amount of packaging is going to alter age, square footage, and location. Undoubtedly, they are influenced by a sharp-looking home, but appraisal reality still applies.

Still, showcasing a home is important. It allows a home to attract offers in the top range of values rather the middle or lower levels. This becomes more important when the market is slowing down or there are a lot of homes in your price range.

The bottom line is if you don't have the time to prep your home, hiring a professional can be a money-making move.

How One Professional Supersizes Closing Checks

Gena Mendez is a professional home stager and an Accredited Staging Professional™ (ASP). Her Utah company, Perfect Impressions, works with homeowners, Realtors, and builders showcasing their homes so they sell faster and for more money. They have an impressive track record in prepping homes that push the right emotional buttons.

According to Mendez and StagedHomes.com a recent study of 2,772 sold properties in eight cities over a six-month period showed staged homes averaged 13.9 days on market compared to 30.9 days for other sold homes. In addition, the staged homes sold for 6.32 percent over list versus 1.6 percent for homes sold without staging. Obviously, this was a hot market because homes were selling over list price.

In a normal market, using a professional would probably be even more advantageous because more homes on the market means more competition.

However, it's interesting to note that in a slower market, as inventories expand, the number of dumpy homes grow and a showcased home will stand out like a frog sitting in the potato salad at a picnic.

In summary, advantages to professionally staging your home are:

1. As an alternative to lowering the price, staging a home will often jumpstart sales and bring in offers. Cutting your price should be "Plan B" only if staging the home doesn't bring results.
2. You'll often net more money by making your home more attractive than discounting the price thousands of dollars.
3. Professionally showcasing the home can cut down on selling time dramatically and improving your bottom line even further.

The following photos illustrate some of the basics of giving your rooms a facelift.

Entryway Before. Entryways are important for creating first impressions. This one lacks visual interest.

Entryway After. A fresh coat of paint and a few added props create the kind of visual interest that beckons a visitor into your home.

Dining Room Before. An unstaged dining area can eliminate your home from serious consideration.

Dining Room After. With the excess furnishings placed in storage and a stylish table setting added, buyers can now envision themselves sitting down to a nice meal.

Kitchen Before. A cluttered kitchen is a turn-off to most buyers. It needs to be packaged to create emotional appeal.

Kitchen After. With the counters and cabinet tops cleaned and the refrigerator magnets removed, the kitchen invites buyers to imagine themselves using it.

Master Bathroom Before. A typical bathroom, not one that will impress buyers comparing it to bathrooms in other homes on the market.

Master Bathroom After. Some delcuttering and new paint make this bathroom more competitive.

Master Bedroom Before. This bedroom will have prospective buyers nodding off.

Master Bedroom After. With clutter and excess furniture gone and a few simple furnishings added, the bedroom is now lively and elegant.

Kids Bedroom Before. This room was cluttered and drab with light yellow paint.

Kids Bedroom Before. It also had countless knickknacks and a dog, who, though cute, could trigger a visitor's allergies.

Kids Bedroom After. The room was transformed with a chair rail, sky blue paint below the rail and white above it. Color matching trim, where the wall meets the ceiling, adds a finished touch.

Kids Bedroom After. Its books were straightened, its knickknacks packed away, and the dog was taken to a neighbor's house.

Home Office. If home offices are common in your area, turn a bedroom into an office and put your home on a buyer's short list.

Second Bathroom Before. An average bathroom, one that buyers will easily forget.

Second Bathroom After. A new light bar and colorful orange and green towels make this bathroom more attractive.

A P P E N D I X 1

Tax Aspects of Making Over Your Home and Selling It

One great perk of doing all the work outlined in this book is that if you've made improvements that increase your basis (add to your home's value), you'll get some tax breaks when you sell.

Typical improvements that increase your basis are:

IMPROVEMENTS THAT GENERALLY ADD VALUE TO YOUR HOME

Additions	Lawn and Grounds	Heating and AC
Bedrooms	Landscaping	Heating system
Baths	Driveway	Central AC
Decks	Walkway	Furnace
Garage	Fences	Duct work
Porch	Retaining wall	Central humidifier
Patio	Sprinkler system	Filter system
Family room	Swimming pool	Efficiency upgrades

(continues)

Plumbing	Interior Improvements	Insulation
Septic system	Built-in appliances	Attic
Water heater	Kitchen remodel	Walls and floor
Soft water system	Flooring upgrades	Pipes and ductwork
Filter system	Central vacuum	
	Wiring upgrades	

Other		
New roof		
Storm windows		
New doors		
Security system		

For tax purposes, repairs that maintain the home in good condition or prolong its life don't add to its value. Examples of these kinds of repairs are:

Repainting the home inside and out

Fixing rain gutters

Repairing walls or ceilings

Replacing carpeting

Fixing floors

Repairing leaks

Replacing broken widows

Any normal maintenance items

Other Tax Considerations When Selling

Currently, the tax code allows an individual $250,000 and a married couple filing jointly $500,000 tax-free when selling a principal residence. A few years ago this didn't seem like a big problem in many areas of the country. However, homes prices have escalated to the point that a lot fewer homeowners will escape going over the limits and having to report capital gains on Schedule D (Form 1040).

When you upgrade and improve your home to sell, keep track of what you do and the receipts. Some of your expenses in showcasing your home may increase your basis and be a tax break.

Even if you have others do your tax return, you should go to www.irs.gov for IRS forms and look at Publication 523, *Selling Your Home*. Other publications that may also affect your tax situation are:

521–Moving Expenses

527–Residential Rental Property

530–Tax Information for First-Time Homeowners

544–Sales and Other Dispositions of Assets

547–Casualties, Disasters, and Thefts

551–Basis of Assets

587–Business Use of Your Home

936–Home Mortgage Interest Deduction

Highlights of the Tax Aspects of Selling Your Home

Some of the main items you'll need to be aware of as a home seller at tax time are:

- The IRS defines your main home as the one you live in most of the time. It can be a house, houseboat, mobile home, cooperative apartment, or condo.

- You must have lived in the home for at least two years of the last five years. If you have more than one home, you can exclude gain only on the sale of your main home, the one you live in most of the time.

- Gain is defined as the selling price (line 101 on the HUD settlement statement). Amount realized is the selling price minus the selling expenses.

- Selling expenses are commissions, advertising, legal fees, and loan charges paid by you for the seller, such as points or closing costs.

- Basis is determined by how you got the home: what it cost if you bought it or the fair market value if you got it by inheritance or gift.

Adjusted basis can be an increase or decrease to your basis depending on what you do to the home or what happens while you own it. Improvements that have a useful life of more than one year generally increase your basis. Credits for losses, energy improvement costs, and so on decrease your basis.

Recordkeeping

Of course, keeping records and receipts of your home improvement projects and the costs you incur prepping your home to sell are critical.

Records you should keep are:

- Proof of the home's purchase price and related costs. (These are all on the HUD Settlement Statement you signed at closing.)
- Keep a specific file for improvements, additions, and other items that affect your adjusted basis—that is, the items that add value. This file may also come in handy as a selling tool to document the cost of improvements to a buyer.
- Keep the worksheets (found in IRS Publication 523) you used to figure adjusted basis when you sell your home.
- Also keep any other worksheets or paperwork related to your home's sale for at least three years or longer if you have postponed gain.
- If you don't live in the home continuously, you need to have proof of the time you did live in it.

One home seller knew he needed to do major work on his home before he would be able to sell it. He also knew it would be a challenge deciding which outlays added to value and which ones wouldn't.

Using Quicken™, an accounting program, the owner was able to keep track of expenses. He also set up a simple system that filed basis-allowable receipts in one folder and nonallowable receipts in another. However, at tax time the owner went over the paperwork with a certified public accountant and fine-tuned what expenses were allowable.

Over the next couple of months, the owner spent nearly $40,000 putting his home in selling shape. He estimated that about $28,500 went to improvements that increased the value or basis of his home and made it salable. The other $11,500 was spent on prepping and packaging costs. In the end, the home sold for top price and netted the owner a nice profit.

Meeting the Use Test

The rules for this are liberal. To take the tax exclusion of a principal residence, all you must do is show that you owned and lived in the property as your main home for either 24 full months or 730 days during the five-year period, which ends on the date of the sale.

Short temporary absences for vacations or other seasonal absences, even if you rent out the property during these times, are counted as periods of use.

If you own a cooperative apartment, you must have owned the stock for at least two years and lived in the apartment for at least two years.

There are exemptions to the above rules if you have to sell due to health, employment, unforeseen circumstances, and so on (see the worksheets in Publication 523).

Keeping Your Home as a Rental

If you can't sell your home in a slow market or you owe more than it's currently worth, renting it until the market improves can be a good strategy.

For example, Dan and Sheila tried to sell their home of twenty years when he got a better job offer in another state. A few months prior, they had refinanced the home and ended up with a loan that was more than they were able to sell their home for.

Not wanting to give up his job offer, Dan and Sheila decided to rent their home for a year or two in hopes of the market improving to where they could break even. They rented the home for over two years and the local market did go up. They were not only able to sell the home but also were able to walk away with a good profit.

Because the owners lived in the home two out of the last five years, they were able to sell the home and not have taxable gain.

Another way to defer taxable gain is with a 1031 exchange. It's not a way to avoid taxes, but a great tool for building equity and transferring it from property to property.

1031 Tax-Deferred Exchanges

This underutilized financial tool can make a big difference in the following situations:

1. You want to keep your starter home for a rental when you move up.

2. If you've rented part of your home and it's subject to capital gains.

3. You want to trade your single family up to a duplex or fourplex.

4. Someone has an investment property (single-family rental, duplex, or even new build job) you would like, but if they sold, capital gains would kick in.

The possibilities are endless for creating win-win deals and deferring capital gains to a time when the tax bite is not so painful.

Unfortunately, paying capital gains taxes keeps many owners from selling single-family homes and condos they've owned for years and would like to unload. These properties may be homes they couldn't sell in a slow market so they've rented them. Eventually, the market changes and suddenly the rental has lots of equity and a growing tax liability.

Not wanting to go through the pain of fixing up the property and putting it on the market, many owners continue living with the problem and procrastinating instead of doing something proactive. As equity grows, the problem grows for many owners.

Luckily, a 1031 exchange may be able to solve their problem by getting them into something more suited to their interests.

Putting an exchange together is fairly straightforward but may require the expertise of an exchange intermediary, accountant, and a title/escrow company depending on the number of properties and complexity. The exchange intermediary is the neutral party that handles the nuts and bolds of the exchange. To find one, look in the yellow pages or check the Internet under "real estate exchange." Or better still, Realtors and title companies who do 1031 exchanges will be able to recommend good intermediaries. You'll also need a title or escrow company to handle title work and funding.

The exciting thing about 1031 exchanges is you don't have to have two property owners who want to exchange straight across; you can bring in other buyers and sellers with their properties to add to the mix.

Here's a simplified example: you find a buyer for the property you want to get rid of (relinquished property) and the sale goes in escrow. You have forty-five days to find a property you want to buy (replacement property) and that goes into the escrow. The buy/sell mix closes and you end up with the property you want. The party with the least equity can use cash or financing to make up the difference.

How One Couple Profited from an Exchange

When Norm and Sandy were transferred from Utah to Georgia the market was slow. They couldn't sell the home they were living in, nor could they sell a smaller rental home they bought from an estate. So they hired a rental company to manage the homes and both rented for close to what the owner's were paying in mortgage payments.

Three years later, interest rates had dropped, the market had improved, so Norm and Sandy decided to sell the homes. Their strategy was to put the proceeds from the sales into a 1031 exchange escrow with a title company in Utah and find a rental property in Georgia. When they closed on the property where they lived, the funds would be released from escrow and used for a down payment. The balance of the purchase price would come from a nonowner occupied mortgage.

Luckily, the tenants in the smaller home wanted to buy it and were able to qualify for the mortgage payments, which were $80 less than their rent payment. The sale closed and the $37,000 proceeds went into the title company exchange department's escrow account.

While the paperwork for the rental sale was going forward, Norm and Sandy were out looking for rentals in their area. The market was tight and they didn't find anything they liked until two weeks after their home in Utah had closed. (The IRS allows 45 days to identify a property and up to 180 days to close the deal.) They made an offer on a two-bedroom condominium in a good area for $185,000 and it was accepted.

The $37,000 in escrow was used for a 20 percent down payment and the balance financed with a nonowner-occupied mortgage. The equity from one rental home in Utah was transferred to Georgia with no capital gains taxes.

Norm and Sandy's other rental has six months to go on a lease. If the tenants can't or don't want to buy it, it'll go on the market and process will be repeated.

As you can see, the 1031 exchange is a great way to transfer equity from one area to another and defer capital gains taxes. If you're in a difficult market, need to move, and can't sell your home, you can rent it until the market improves and still build equity.

Rules for a 1031 Exchange

The IRS requires the exchange to be like-kind, and it identifies that as real estate for real estate. You can exchange a duplex for bare land, office building, warehouse, or whatever. Just so it's real estate that is not used as a primary or secondary residence.

From the date of closing on the sale of the relinquished property, you have 45 days to find the replacement property(s) and 180 days to close.

You must insert a clause into all sale contracts that identify the transactions as a 1031 exchange. The IRS needs to see an easy-to-follow paper trail.

John and Angie went the exchange route when they decided they no longer wanted the demands of being a landlord. They owned a duplex that had about $80,000 equity and didn't want to pay out a big part of their equity in taxes. Although they didn't want to exchange for more rental property, undeveloped land appeared to be a good way to go because there is low maintenance, and no rent to collect or late-night plumbing problems to fix.

Finding a buyer for their duplex was easy and the sale closed with the proceeds going into escrow. Their Realtor found a ten-acre parcel for sale that appeared to be in the path of eventual development.

Since the land cost $139,000, John and Angie needed about $59,000 to make a deal. They decided to take out a ten-year, low-interest equity line of credit on their home for the funds needed to complete the deal. The second leg of the 1031 exchange closed and everyone was happy.

As a result of the exchange, a young couple starting out was able to buy a duplex they had been searching for. John and Angie won't

For more information on 1031 exchanges check out www.firstamex.com or go to irs.gov and download Publication 544 and Form 8824.

have to collect rents or do maintenance on their day off. Everyone wins and the tax man has to wait for another day to collect his due.

TYPICAL STEPS TO A 1031 TAX-DEFERRED EXCHANGE

STEPS	WHAT'S INVOLVED
List property for sale and line up a property exchange intermediary. The intermediary can be a title company or attorney who is experienced in exchanges.	Include a notice in the listing and sales documents that the property is part of a 1031 exchange. As a seller you will assign the role of grantee or transferee of the deed to the intermediary.
A buyer for property is found.	The intermediary prepares an assignment assigning the role of seller to the intermediary, along with the other exchange paperwork, which goes to the closing agent.
The sale is closed and equity funds are put in escrow.	Exchanger and buyer sign assignment agreement, which assigns to the intermediary the role of seller in the sale. The forty-five-day clock starts ticking on identifying an exchange property.
The hunt for a replacement property should be well on its way by this time.	Forty-five days to find property and identify it in writing by street address or legal description. This is faxed to the intermediary.
Exchanger makes an offer on the property.	Included in the purchase agreement is a notice that the deal is part of a 1031 exchange with the required assignments. This usually is not a problem with the sellers, they just want their money and to be on their way.
If there are multiple properties and multiple exchangers.	All the legs of the exchange are put into escrow and closed with each party getting it's designated property at the about the same time. Closing and funding has to be within the 180 days.
File tax forms.	Exchangers file Form 8824 with the IRS and any other state-required forms.

In another case, an investor had several rental homes that he and a friend had owned for several years and the values had increased substantially along with the tenant headaches. Wanting to get rid of these headaches and buy some land, they found a ten-acre parcel that had promise of going up in value over the next few years.

The owners made an offer on the land subject to their rental properties selling over the next sixty days. However, the landowner had been thinking the deal over and decided he wanted to be a landlord so he offered to take one of the homes as a part of the deal. That left three homes that needed to be sold and the proceeds escrowed for a 1031 exchange.

Everything went as planned, the threes homes sold, and the exchange closed. The former landlords ended up with a parcel of land where the only upkeep was cutting the weeds once a month.

As you can see, exchanges are a great way of turning a stale real estate investment into something more exciting for all parties with the taxes deferred.

APPENDIX 2

The Seven Dumbest Mistakes Sellers Make

Dumb Mistake #1:
Not Pricing Your Home at Market Value

When Terri and Ryan put their home on the market they took their mortgage balance, added in estimated closing costs, and the $67,000 they needed to get into their next home. Totaling up these figures they came up with $376,000 for a sales price.

With a lot of hope, they planted a "For Sale" sign in the lawn, put an ad in the local weekly, and waited for a buyer to come by with an open checkbook.

The first weekend went by and nothing happened. After three more weekends with only a couple of lookers and lots of calls from agents, the sellers felt they had better talk to a professional. Time was getting short and their new home would be finished in two months.

Terri's sister had just sold her home and was happy with the results, so Terri called her sister's agent and asked him to come over and look at their home. The agent sat down with Ryan and Terri and went over what other similar homes had sold for in their area the last couple of months. Those comparisons showed homes like theirs sold for $345,000 to $358,000 with an average sales time of thirty-three days. Also, looking at comparable homes currently for sale showed twenty-seven listings within a mile radius.

Most of the homes in the area were built around 2000 and many buyers were first-time owners. After six years, enough of these buyers were starting to move up that the inventory of unsold was growing. That meant the seller's home had a lot of competition that could get worse as spring turned into summer.

By looking at what homes had sold for and factoring in the large number of homes currently for sale, the Realtor suggested a sales price of $349,900. This was $26,100 less than the sellers needed to get. Plus, they had only sixty days until their new home would be finished.

So what happened? Ryan and Terri, upset over the dash of cold reality, cancelled their build job with the builder and lost their $8,000 deposit. Their qualifying ratios were so tight that without a net $60,000 from the sale of their home, they couldn't buy the new one.

To avoid making a dumb mistake pricing your home, you should:

1. Have a Realtor pull up a list of what similar homes have sold for in your area the last month or two. If it's a hot market, only look at the last week or two. You should look at:

   • The list price versus the sales price. Hot market sales prices are often more than list prices. This gives you an idea of how much over the last sales price you can go. A cooling market is the opposite. The wider the gap between list price and sales price, the cooler the market and the longer it usually takes to sell.

   • Homes that are comparable to yours: two-story versus two-story, ranch versus ranch, and so on.

   • Days on market (DOM) or how long it takes homes like yours to sell.

   • The number of homes out there competing with your home.

2. If you don't know an agent, pay a few hundred dollars and hire a certified appraiser. For Ryan and Terri, this would have been far cheaper than losing their $8,000 deposit.

The bottom line reality (good or bad) is your home's worth floats with a changing market that's determined by what similar homes are selling for.

Dumb Mistake #2:
Not Decluttering Your Home

Clutter is to selling a home like obesity is to a Miss America contestant. It isn't going to help your cause if buyers looking at your home are turned off by piles of clutter.

Remember, people buy on emotion. They're looking for a house that evokes hearth and home emotions. For that to happen, buyers must see themselves living in and enjoying the home.

These are also the people who pay full price and don't lowball your price. They want the home and wouldn't think of jeopardizing their chances of getting it, especially in a hot market where competing offers are the norm.

In one case, a woman just about lost her overdecorated home because she thought everyone would appreciate her taste. Her home was a newer ranch in a good area, but she had truckloads of knick-knacks. Every square foot of wall space had a picture, knick-knack, minishelf with a stuffed animal or doll. Glass-fronted cabinets with figurines were everywhere.

People looking at the home were there so enthralled with all the decorations and bric-a-brac that they forgot why they were there. Buyers walked through the home and out the front door talking about all the stuff, the floor plan and home's amenities already forgotten.

Many people went through the home the first two months, but no offers were made. Time was running out. The husband, transferred to another state, struggled with house payments and apartment rent. Since they didn't have much equity, they considered letting the home go into foreclosure.

Eventually, the seller's friend talked her into calling Sandy, an agent who had a great track record selling homes in the area.

When Sandy walked through the home, she was flabbergasted at the amount of stuff the owner had. Obviously, a lot had to change before the home would sell.

The first thing the agent did was to sit down with the owner and talk frankly about what needed to happen. With the owner's commitment, Sandy walked through the home with the owner and worked up a plan of action, along with a checklist of what needed to go. It wasn't a short list.

Basically, Sandy's plan of action was:

- Everything on the walls must go, except for a picture or two.
- Empty the cabinets, box-up the figurines, and move both into storage.
- Excess furniture should go into storage. Leave a couch, love seat, a couple of end tables, coffee table, lamps, and dining set.
- No appliances on the kitchen counter and remove the dozens of refrigerator magnets.
- All the golf and bowling trophies must go. You want to sell the home, not distract a fellow golfer or bowler.

A week later the home was completely different. Tiny, cramped rooms appeared to double in size. It now looked like the 1,400 square feet it was.

The nitty-gritty bottom line here is that you have to move all the stuff out of your home so buyers can visualize themselves living there. You don't want any distractions that break their focus.

Dumb Mistake #3:
Not Taking Care of Problems Upfront

The most important proactive thing you can do in selling your home is to get a professional home inspection upfront. The second proactive thing you should do is set up a plan of action to take care of the things your home inspector found that need to be fixed or replaced.

Some sellers create huge problems by not disclosing problems they know about. They hope buyers won't find out, but they always do and a lawsuit can result.

It's almost certain when buyers make an offer that it's going to be subject to a professional inspector trained to go through the home with a fine-toothed comb. Any undisclosed problems are going to surface. This can kill a promising sale fast because buyers lose confidence in the condition of the home. When that happens it's an off-the-edge-of-the-table plunge for that deal.

Even when the seller offers to take care of the problems, it's often not enough to rekindle the buyer's interest. Remember, buyers run strong on emotion.

Here are some tips on how to avoid losing buyers:

1. Fill out your state's disclosure form completely. If in doubt, explain past problems and how they've been taken care of. Use specifics on what caused the problem, what was done about it, and what materials were used.
2. Don't try to sell a house "as is" to get around problems you know about. You'll have trouble getting financing and buyers may still come back and sue you. If the home is a true dump, work with an attorney to put together paperwork that will protect you from future liability.
3. Hire a reputable home inspector (see yellow pages under "home inspectors") to inspect your home before it goes on the market. You can then use the inspection report as a marketing tool. Show buyers upfront that the home is in good condition. If the inspector finds problems, fix or replace them, and have the report updated. Spending about $300 in the beginning can save bucks later on in the sales process.

Dumb Mistake #4:
Not Prepping and Packaging Your Home

An all-too-common mistake home sellers make is to simply pound a "For Sale" sign in the turf and wait. True, this approach sometimes brings an offer, but how many thousands of dollars does the seller lose when they could have gotten more?

To sell a home for the most money, it has to be properly marketed. Like anything else in sales, it's the packaging that brings in bigger bucks.

In one example of packaging, a couple had tried to sell their home for three months. They had shown it many times, and no one had made an offer. People would walk through quickly and leave, often without pausing to ask questions or make comments.

The sellers were clueless. After three months they started to panic and called Lori, an agent their neighbor recommended.

Walking through the home, the agent could see why the home wasn't selling. It was obvious. The oak floors were dull and scuffed and the walls needed paint bad. Appliances, boxes, and dishes covered the kitchen counters and the chipped sink was full of dirty dishes. The rest of the house was in similar condition. It wasn't a home anyone would want to buy unless they were looking for a fixer-upper.

Lori sat down with the sellers and worked up a "to do" list of repairs that would make the house attractive and salable. However, the sellers refused to do the items on the list. They just wanted to sell as-is and get out of town.

When Lori couldn't get the sellers to budge on doing the repairs, she told them she couldn't help them and walked away from a potential listing. She had learned the hard way before about trying to sell a "junker" property for market value.

When the sellers couldn't sell the home, they rented it and moved several states away. About two months after that, the renters skipped out and left an even bigger mess. Eventually, the home went into foreclosure and the sellers lost about $40,000 in equity and took a big ding on their credit.

Although this is an extreme case, there are vital lessons we can glean from this example that can help you avoid costly mistakes:

- If you want to sell your home *as is*, market your home to fixer-upper or investor buyers. They usually pay cash, (no appraisers, no bank rules) but discount the price heavily. You'll get a lot more money if you fix it up first.

  Also, if a mortgage lender is involved, the home has to be appraised. If the appraiser comes back with a list of repairs, you're back where you started. It's best to invest time and money putting the home in good selling condition first. You'll usually get $5 to $10 back for every dollar you spend prepping your home.

- Look around the neighborhood and see what other homeowners have done. You want your home to look just a tad better. Buyers buy into a neighborhood first, and if your home fits in you'll attract the buyer who pays at or close to list price.

- Don't try to cut corners by offering a painting or carpeting allowance. If your home needs paint and floor coverings, buyers will frequently make low offers and want the allowance too.

- Once buyers find something wrong, their thinking goes into "what else is wrong," quickly followed by "how cheap can we get the house for," as they sharpen their pencil.

- One of the key themes of this book is most people buy homes on emotion. The more you appeal to their emotions, the less price becomes an issue. If your home is prepped and packaged to sell, you'll likely get a full-price offer.

Dumb Mistake #5: Not Lining Up Your Ducks Before Planting the Sign

Twelve months ago, Lorin and Carol bought their first home with an interest-only loan. Their lender convinced them this was the way to go because the home's appreciation would build equity faster than paying down the loan. Then a job opportunity came along in their home town where they could be closer to family. It was too good to pass up, so they put their home on the market.

A week later the home sold and the transaction headed for closing. The sellers figured they would get enough money from the sale to put a good down payment on their next home.

Come closing day, the sellers sat at the closing table and looked over the HUDs. On line 508 of the sellers column was a prepayment penalty for $6,240. The sellers had forgotten that if they paid off the loan or refinanced the first three years, they would be charged a penalty.

So what should the sellers have done to avoid this? Actually, they may not have been able to avoid it, but they should have contacted their lender before putting their home on the market for a payoff and any other costs. The closing table is not the place for surprises.

Other stress-inducing situations are:

- Sellers who wait to put their home on the market when buying a new home so they won't have to move twice. This can cause major stress if the home doesn't sell by the new home's closing date. Many buyers' deposits are lost because they don't plan for the worst case scenario. It's better to give yourself plenty of time to sell the home and line up a relative or rental in case the home sells quickly.

- Pets: You may love your dogs, cats, tropical snakes, and so on, but buyers who don't like animals or have allergies will make a fast U-turn out the home if they're there. It's likely any agent who has sold more than two homes can relate horror stories of pets or pet smells killing potential sales. If you have pets, make arrangements to board them or have a neighbor pet-sit while showing the home.

- Sellers who put their home on the market subject to finding another home. If you do this, you'll discourage serious buyers from considering your home. Buyers won't want to wait around for you to find another house.

  If this is a concern for you and the market is fairly hot, try finding a home and making an offer subject to your home selling. Perhaps the seller of the home you want needs a longer time to move and it could be a win-win. True, this is a weak approach but it beats discouraging buyers from making offers on your home.

- Legal matters, such as divorce, death, liens, or judgments can affect the title. It's vital to get them completely cleaned up before putting the home on the market.

  One problem that can have a few fireworks attached is when there has been a divorce and the ex-spouses's name is still on the title. When the house sells, the ex-spouse decides that now is the time for payback and refuses to sign a quit-claim deed or whatever is needed to complete the sale. If there's any doubt about clear title, get with an attorney and clean it up before planting the sign.

Dumb Mistake #6:
Not Making Sure the Buyer Is Preapproved

The agent had barely sat down when the sellers started telling of their discouraging experience. Nearly four months ago, a young buyer came by in response to their ad and wanted to make an offer. He told them he would go full price if they would work with him. Not thinking too much about it, they signed a purchase agreement and waited for it to close.

Weeks went by and they finally called the buyer who told them he was having some delays but it should be soon. More weeks went by and the sellers finally contacted the buyer's lender. He told them there were a few problems but they could be worked out and to be patient.

After another month, they called the lender and he said basically the same thing. It was a string-along. Eventually both buyer and lender stopped returning phone calls and after another month, the sellers concluded the buyer was no longer interested and willing to forfeit his measly $25 earnest money.

Now their new home was a month away from completion and panic started to creep in. The home would have to be priced low market to attract a fast sale, there was no time to go for top dollar.

The home did sell quickly but for thousands of dollars less than it would have if the sellers had had more time.

Lessons learned:

- Never consider an offer unless there's a preapproval letter attached from a mortgage lender.
- Don't sign an offer until you've talked to the buyer's lender and verified the buyers are really preapproved.
- Insist on a deposit big enough to make it painful for buyers to back out and big enough to compensate you for the time your home was off the market.

Also make sure the time you give buyers to complete inspections, appraisals, and other deadlines is no more than ten days. Preapproved buyers don't need more than that if they're working with a reasonably competent lender.

Not preapproving your buyer can bite especially hard if you're buying a home too and trying to close both the same time. A glitch on the selling end a few days before closing can have costly consequences, such as:

- An appraisal comes in low and you scramble to keep the buyer from walking away. Rather than risk the deal by trying to get the numbers up, you lower the price.
- The buyer suddenly finds they're short enough money to close. Since you're a day or two away from closing, you agree to pay a few thousand dollars of their closing costs.
- A credit or income problem surfaces that jeopardizes the buyer's loan. The lender scrambles to find alternative financing that ends up costing you in points or additional closing costs if you want to keep the deal together.

The bottom line is always verify the buyer's prequalification letter and keep a short leash on the purchase agreement's conditions, inspections, and deadlines.

Dumb Mistake #7:
Putting Your Home on the Market Before It's Ready

Many owners put their home up for sale with little planning or research. They hear that a house down the block sold for a certain amount and go with that price. Others may feel their home is much better and tack on a few thousand dollars—a surcharge for nice decorating or landscaping.

Other times, sellers try to avoid doing homework by "testing" the market to see if someone will come along and give them their price. If they don't sell, then maybe they'll talk to a Realtor.

Putting your home on the market before you've done the homework can result in some negative consequences. Here are some of the more common ones.

- At any one time, there is a finite buyer pool who can afford your home. If you're overpriced, these buyers eliminate your home from their list and it may take weeks or months before new buyers replace them. If you lower your price, buyers have already eliminated you and it may take awhile for them to overcome their rejection. This means you can easily double your selling time.

- Putting your home on the market before you've decluttered and showcased it to sell can bite you. Hoping to sell it while you're doing the prep work can also bite you. You don't want to deplete that buyer pool so when your home is ready to sell, they've already seen it and moved on.

- Telling a buyer that you want an offer subject to finding another home can kill a deal. If this condition is on the listing, most agents won't even show it. If you need a bigger home, go out and find it and make an offer subject to your home selling. If that seller goes along with it, great for you. Otherwise, the best strategy is sell your home, bank the money, and rent a place so you can house hunt without pressure.

- Get title problems cleaned up before putting the home on the market. Few things irritate agents and buyers more than making an offer and finding out there are problems that delay a closing.

- Selling a home you've rented out to uncooperative tenants can deplete a buyer pool fast. If it's listed, agents will avoid it like the latest mutated virus. Better to wait until the tenants move out then clean and prep it. You'll make a lot more money going this route.

Index

Accredited Staging Professionals (ASPs),
    175
  advantages of using, 177
  fee schedule, 176
  sources of, 175
ads
  choosing the right medium, 130–131
  creating the message, 129–130
  on the Internet, 131
  sample, 130
agents
  advantages of using, 121–123
  characteristics to look for, 12
  checking out showcasing skills of, 19
  choosing the right, 4, 20, 122
  need for experience, 122–123
amenities, as component of valuation,
    21–22
appliances
  life expectancy, 71–72
  need for matching colors, 62–63
appointment calls, screening of,
    134–136

appraisals
  and concessions, 8–9
  Fannie Mae guidelines for, 7, 9
  inflated, 8
  low, 146–147
  process, 7–11
appreciation rate, 16
"as is" sales
  options for handling, 160
  problems created by, 159, 201
  selling to investors, 202
attic, decluttering of, 39

backyard, 117–118
  prepping for sale, 119
basements
  cleaning of, 51
  cost of finishing, 74
  decluttering of, 39
bathrooms
  cleaning of, 49
  decluttering of, 33

bathrooms (*continued*)
    prepping to sell, 112–113
    repair checklist, 63
    showcasing of, 180–181, 185
    use of lighting in, 113
bedrooms
    cleaning of, 50
    colors for, 67
    decluttering of, 34
    prepping to sell, 114–115
    showcasing of, 181–184
bushes and shrubs, increasing curb appeal with, 98
buyers
    importance of listening to, 154
    professional shoppers, 142–143
    turn-offs for, 105
buyer's market
    advantage of realtors in, 155
    for condo sales, 171–173
    importance of timing in, 155–156
    pot sweeteners in, 153
    reasons for, 152–153

carpeting
    avoiding allowance, 203
    replacement options, 74
cats
    hiding the litter box, 33, 36
    removal during home showing, 33
cleaning
    economic advantages, 43–44
    investing in a service, 42–43
    websites, 45
    when to start, 44
cleaning checklist
    for bathroom, 49
    for bedrooms, 50
    for kitchen, 47–48
    for living room, 45–46
cleaning services
    considerations, 54
    costs, 55
    options for, 53
    websites, 54
clients, feedback from, 5

closets
    cleaning of, 50
    decluttering of, 36–37
    organizers for, 36–37
closing costs, paying the buyer's, 153
closing date
    deadline, 145
    extension, 154
clutter, *see also* decluttering
    as turn-off for buyers, 105, 199–200
colors, keeping them simple, 107–108
comparables
    comparison worksheet, 14
    lack of, 9
    in residential appraisal, 10
comparative market analysis (CMA), 4
    proactive nature of, 11
competition, as component of valuation, 6, 21
condition of home, as component of valuation, 6, 21–22
condos
    financing rules, 171–172
    ownership ratio, 172
    tips for selling, 172–173
contingencies, list of common, 148–149
contractors
    finding the right, 88–89
    sorting through the bids, 89
counteroffers, 145–149
    and low appraisals, 146–147
    and price, 146
curb appeal, *see also* landscaping; prepping your home to sell
    checklist for increasing, 97–98
    first impressions as key, 26–27, 92
    importance of, 24–27, 91–94
    using photographs to check, 24–25
    worksheet, 25

days on market (DOM), 15
    impact on salability, 4–5
    as pulse of area's housing market, 17
deadlines
    danger of extending, 147
    as key in offers, 144
    for purchase contract, 145

deck
  cost of adding, 80
  prepping for sale, 117
  upgrading of, 84
declining market, sales techniques in, 17–18
decluttering
  action plan for, 200
  avoid overdecorating, 199
  defined, 28
  moving stuff into storage, 30
  worksheet for, 30–31
decluttering worksheet
  for bathroom, 33
  for bedroom, 34
  for kitchen, 32–33
  for living room, 30–31
decorating allowance, downside of, 61
default, programs for avoiding, 162
dining room
  prepping to sell, 111
  showcasing of, 178–179
disclosure form, 201
divorce
  ensuring clear title, 204
  sales options during, 164–166
dog, cleaning up after, 39
down payment
  bigger is better, 152
  creative ideas for, 154
drainage problems, 100–101
Dress Your House for Success video, 167
driveway, increasing curb appeal, 98

electrical work
  cost of upgrading, 74
  repairs, 63
entertainment center, 116
entryway, prepping to sell, 108–109

family room
  cost of adding, 74, 80
  decluttering of, 116–117
  prepping to sell, 115–117
Fannie Mae (Federal National Mortgage Association), guidelines for appraisers, 7, 9

fireplace, prepping of, 115
floors, when to replace, 62
flyer boxes, 125
flyers
  to hand out during garage sale, 132
  key points to convey, 127
  sample, 128
  for targeting buyers, 126–127
foreclosure
  effect on credit rating, 163–164, 166
  selling a house in, 166–168
forsalebyowner.com, 3
front yard, prepping to sell, 108
FSBO, *see* selling by owner
furniture placement
  in bedrooms, 114–115
  decorating websites, 114
  in family room, 116
  in living room, 109–110

garages
  avoid using for storage, 40
  decluttering of, 37–38
  degreasing of, 38
  detached, 85
  finishing of unfinished, 38
  replacing of doors, 84

handrails, 84
home
  getting a sense of, 12–13
  packaging, *see* prepping your home to sell
  seeing it as others would, 27–28
  showcasing your, 175–185
  value of, *see* valuation
home improvements, *see also* upgrades
  value-adding, 187–188
  vs. repairs, 188
home inspections
  deadline for, 145
  need for upfront, 200–201
  as potential deal killers, 147–148
home inspectors
  reasons for hiring, 60
  websites for, 59
  working with upfront, 201

home office
  cost of adding, 74, 80
  showcasing of, 184
home warranty, 154
hot market, *see* seller's market
house exterior
  cleaning of, 51–55
  cost *vs.* value of upgrades, 78–79
  fix-up checklist, 83–85
  hiring a cleaning service, 53–55
  key fix-up items, 83
  problems inspectors look for, 102
How to Prepare Your Home for Sale
    video, 167
HUDs (financial statement), 163, 164

inspections, *see* home inspections
IRS publications, 188–189

kitchen
  cleaning checklist, 47–48
  cost of upgrading, 15
  decluttering of, 31–33
  as focal point of home, 48
  prepping to sell, 106, 111–112
  showcasing of, 179–180

landscaping
  checklist, 97–98
  importance of, 92–93
  plan of action for, 94–97
  websites, 96
laundry room
  decluttering of, 35–36
  repair checklist, 63
lawn
  mowing, 96
  regular maintenance, 96
  seeding *vs.* sod, 95–96
  using lawn-care companies, 95
light fixtures, cleaning of, 47
living room
  cleaning checklist, 45–46
  colors used in, 67, 109, 110
  decluttering of, 30
  furniture arrangement, 110
  prepping to sell, 109

loans
  deadline for application, 145
  deadline for denial, 145
loan-to-value (LTV) mortgage, 164, 165
location
  as component of valuation, 5–6, 21
  as key in determining value, 11

mildew, *see* mold
mold
  hints for finding, 64
  removal of, 63–65
Morrill, Judy, 61
multiple offers, 149–152, *see also* offers
  procedure for dealing with, 150
  worksheet for comparisons, 151–152
multiple listing service (MLS), 2

National Association of Home Inspec-
    tors, 100
National Association of Realtors, *Profile
    of Home Buyers and Sellers,* 121
"no shoes in house" rule, 45

offer comparison worksheet, 151–152
offers, *see also* multiple offers
  with contingencies, 148–149
  deadline for acceptance, 145
  deadlines as key in, 144
  options for dealing with, 143–144
  "upon presentation" clause, 156
open houses
  advertising for, 140
  food options for, 141
  during holidays, 139
  tips for, 140–141

packaging to sell, *see* prepping your home
    to sell
painting
  appealing to the broadest tastes, 66
  avoiding allowance, 66, 203
  of ceilings, 68
  "how to" suggestions, 67–68
  need for neutral colors, 65–66
  quality brands, 67
  websites, 68

patios
prepping for sale, 117–118
upgrading of, 84
pets, making arrangements for, 33, 204
plumbing repairs, 63
porch, upgrading of, 84, 85
possession, deadline for, 145
preapproval letters
importance of, 205
need to verify, 144, 206
problem with, 60–61
prepayment penalties, 155, 203
prepping your home to sell, 106–108, *see also* showcasing your home
bathroom, 112–113
bedroom, 114–115
dining room, 111
family room, 115
importance of, 21, 201–203
as key in making the sale, 201–203
kitchen, 106, 111–112
living room, 109
pressure cleaners, tips for using, 51–52
price
as component of valuation, 6, 21
and counteroffers, 146
disclosure of, 13
pricing
doing the homework, 4
failure to price to market value, 197–198
key considerations, 198
list *vs.* sale price, 198
Profile of Home Buyers and Sellers (NAR), 121

realtor.com, 3
referrals, 131–132
remodels, *see* upgrades
rental
1031 exchange, *see* 1031 exchange
keeping home as, 191
repairclinic.com, 31
repairs
allowing time for, 58
of bathroom, 63
defined, 57

electric, 63
fix-it checklist, 62–63
identification of, 58–60
vs. upgrades, 57
roof
need for inspection, 84
replacement of, 79, 80

sales prices, *see* price; pricing
scams, 86–87
tips for avoiding, 87–88
second story, cost of adding, 80–81
security precautions, when showing your home, 133–134
seller disclosures, deadline for, 145
seller's market
as component of valuation, 6
monthly appreciation rate, 16
selling by owner
advantages of, 123–124
advertising, 129–131
flyer boxes, 125
flyers, 126–129
referrals, 131–132
use of signs, 124–125
vs. use of agents, 121–122
selling your home
in "as is" condition, 158–160
during a divorce, 164–166
doing the homework, 206–207
relevant tax publications, 188–189
use test, 190–191
when facing foreclosure, 166–168
when property is stigmatized, 168–171
septic systems, presale suggestions, 85–86
short sales
causes of, 160
defined, 160
options for handling, 161, 162–164
sales package for, 163
showcasing your home, *see also* Accredited Staging Professionals (ASPs); curb appeal
before-after examples, 177–185
using professionals, 175–176

showing your home
  with an agent, 138–139
  during holidays, 139
  likely questions, 137–138
  screening calls, 134–136
  security precautions, 133–134
  tips for, 136–138
siding
  cost of replacement, 80
  cost *vs.* value, 84
signs, design and purpose of, 124–125
slow market, *see* buyer's market
Speed Cleaning (Dellutri), 44
stigmatized properties
  common causes, 169
  disclosure required, 168, 170
  overcoming the problem, 171
storage
  choosing a site, 40
  insuring the contents, 40
  preventing damage during, 40–41
sun room, cost of adding, 80
swimming pool, prepping for sale, 118,
  119

tax-deferred exchange, *see* 1031 tax-
  deferred exchange
tax implications
  capital gains, 188, 189, 192
  tax basis, 189
  tracking expenses, 190
  use test, 190–191
1031 tax-deferred exchange, 191–192
  examples, 192–193, 195–196

rules for, 194
typical steps, 195
tile, used in kitchen, 111–112
title, resolving problems with, 207
turn-offs for buyers, 105

Uniform Residential Appraisal Report,
  10
upgrades
  benefits of, 57–58
  cost *vs.* value, 70–71, 73
  defined, 57
  planning chart, 73–74
  vs. repairs, 57
use test, 190–191

valuation
  comparison worksheet, 14
  components of, 5–6

walkways, 84
wallpaper stripping
  suggestions, 68–69
  website, 69
water problems, 100–101
wells, presale suggestions, 86
window-cleaning
  for hard-water stains, 53
  supplies, 53
  techniques, 52
windows
  cost of replacement, 80
  upgrading of, 84
word-of-mouth advertising, 44

yard, decluttering of, 38–39

Look for These Exciting Real Estate Titles at
www.amacombooks.org/go/realestate

A Survival Guide for Buying a Home by Sid Davis $17.95

A Survival Guide for Selling a Home by Sid Davis $15.00

Are You Dumb Enough to Be Rich? by G. William Barnett II $18.95

Everything You Need to Know Before Buying a Co-op, Condo, or Townhouse by Ken Roth $18.95

Home Makeovers That Sell by Sid Davis $15.00

Make Millions Selling Real Estate by Jim Remley $18.95

Mortgages 101 by David Reed $16.95

Mortgage Confidential by David Reed $16.95

Real Estate Investing Made Simple by M. Anthony Carr $17.95

Real Estate Presentations That Make Millions by Jim Remley $18.95

The Complete Guide to Investing in Foreclosures by Steve Berges $17.95

The Consultative Real Estate Agent by Kelle Sparta $17.95

The Home Buyer's Question and Answer Book by Bridget McCrea $16.95

The Landlord's Financial Tool Kit by Michael C. Thomsett $18.95

The Property Management Tool Kit by Mike Beirne $19.95

The Real Estate Agent's Business Planner by Bridget McCrea $19.95

The Real Estate Agent's Field Guide by Bridget McCrea $19.95

The Real Estate Investor's Pocket Calculator by Michael C. Thomsett $17.95

The Successful Landlord by Ken Roth $19.95

Who Says You Can't Buy a Home! by David Reed $17.95

Your Successful Real Estate Career, Fifth Edition, by Kenneth W. Edwards $18.95

Available at your local bookstore, online, or call 800-250-5308
Savings start at 35% on Bulk Orders of 5 copies of more!
Save up to 55%!
For details, contact AMACOM Special Sales
Phone: 212-903-8316. E-mail: SpecialSls@amanet.org